Picking Up the Pieces

Stories of Encouragement for Mending Hearts

Gracie Thompson

TEACH Services, Inc.
PUBLISHING
www.TEACHServices.com • (800) 367-1844

Copyright © 2015 TEACH Services, Inc.
ISBN-13: 978-1-4796-0478-4 (Paperback)
ISBN-13: 978-1-4796-0479-1 (ePub)
ISBN-13: 978-1-4796-0480-7 (Mobi)
Library of Congress Control Number: 2015933650

Published by

TEACH Services, Inc.
P U B L I S H I N G
www.TEACHServices.com • (800) 367-1844

Table of Contents

Introduction

There is no greater pain on this earth than the tragic, sudden death of one's child. It is a blind side that one is never prepared for, and it shatters the heart. After my son's death, I took comfort in God's Word, especially Psalm 34:18 and Jeremiah 17:14. As part of the grieving and healing process, I began writing down my thoughts. God knew I needed to put down words, feeble though they may be, to the pain I was experiencing. Writing has been cathartic, and I highly recommend it. I can look back and see the value of purging pain in words, which started me on the path of healing. Of course, this healing will only be finished when He returns. Until I draw my last breath, I will miss and grieve for my son. But reaching out to help another in anguish blesses both the giver and receiver.

I enjoy blogging and post weekly on a variety of grief sites on social media. I have heard of other authors turning their blogs into books, and I decided to pursue that idea in hopes of helping others who are living with loss and sadness. Sometimes lines from an old hymn will provide a needed blessing. Other times a Bible story will smooth the rough edges of one's day. There are countless ways to reach out and touch another human being with the hands, feet, and heart of Jesus, and I have selected some stories to share with you.

As you pause to read each page, it is my prayer that you will take away the central theme that we have hope—hope in a God who loves us and understands our pain, whether we are grieving from the loss of a child to disease, a parent to old age, a friend to suicide, or a spouse to an accident. Death is unavoidable in this sinful world, but we have hope through a risen Savior and the assurance of His soon return.

For those who have lost a loved one, especially a loved one to suicide, healing is what we seek. It is not instant, and it cannot be rushed. It is also my opinion that restoration is not complete without including God in the process. God has called me to reach out to those who are suffering similar pain as I am. If I can help by giving voice to the unique grieving that one goes through who has lost someone to suicide, then I have completed the task that God has given me. It is hard to fathom, but every forty seconds someone in the world completes suicide. That adds up to at least one million annually. Do the math and you quickly realize how many families and friends are left with an empty hole in their hearts that only God can repair. By His amazing grace, He fashions us anew.

God Sent Pipy

We never know where life's journey will take us, and many have been sideswiped by tragedy. Seemingly out of thin air we are forced to accept that our journey forward will be laced with grief and take on a life of its own. Long before I became an author and blogger, I wrote this story. I didn't date it (somehow I always think I will remember), but it was written a few months after my son died. Searching through some papers recently, I came across it. I sat back and read it again, allowing it to transport me back to another time when my life was innocent and fair. Here's the beginning of my life with Pipy in it. May you enjoy the story whether you are a feline lover or not.

One warm evening last summer my husband and I took a stroll down our country road. On the right side was a huge soybean field, lush and green from the abundant rain. Suddenly we heard a faint mew. It sounded like a kitten. We stopped and stared in the direction of the sound. A tiny kitten peeked through the foliage, a skinny little gray tiger kitten. *Poor thing.* I thought. *Perhaps he has been looking for food in the field?* He was not afraid of us and wanted to be held. We already had a cat, a spoiled unfriendly Samantha. But this kitten could use one good meal at least.

It was useless to put him down. He was not going back where he came from. He dogged our steps, so it was either pick him up or step on him. All the way home I pondered the options: did he have an owner who missed him? Unlikely, since we were surrounded by horse farms with barns and probably dozens of nameless cats. Was he tossed out to fend for himself? Perhaps, but he was not fearful at all. At least we could feed him before sending him back out to live on his own. One look at the way my husband held him gave me an inkling that this kitten's chances had already improved.

He ate like the starved kitten he was. And as he did, he began to work himself into our hearts. Soon we were trying to think of names for this "outdoor mouser." No way could he be inside with Sammy. I don't know where the name Pipy came from, but he just seemed like a tiny pipsqueak, so small and frail. Soon he responded to his name and would come bouncing up to me from wherever his explorations took him.

Pipy is a kind and gentle kitten. He loves to play and has large almond-shaped expressive eyes. He soon won over our hearts to the point that there was talk about making him an indoor cat, considering the cold winter soon to come. Gradually, we introduced Pipy to Sammy, and to this day she snarls at him, but they seem to get along like any other siblings.

Little did we know that the fun antics from this kitten would soothe our broken hearts. Within weeks we became shocked and grieving parents when our oldest son ended his life. There are no words to express the anguish this created in our hearts. Perhaps time will help us learn to live again. Each day we shed buckets of tears that only God sees. We know that He is traveling this dark road with us.

During those first long and painful weeks, it began to dawn on us that perhaps God sent Pipy to us. He knew that our lives would soon be turned upside down and we would need this fun-loving kitten to ease our pain and bring out peals of laughter in the midst of our grief. Each time we find ourselves laughing at this silly kitten, we remind ourselves that God does care about the simplest things because He gave us a "baby" to love.

We could fill a book with Pipy's antics. He is fascinated with the concept of gravity. He loves to push things off the edge of any surface and watch them drop to the floor. Needless to say, it is not unlike picking up after a child again. He and Sammy get into rough and tumble fights. Pipy is obviously having the time of his life. Sammy? Not so much. She hates having her calm and peaceful world so radically disrupted, so she hisses and growls at him, which of course fascinates him and makes us laugh.

One morning I heard what sounded like thundering hooves tearing up and down the hallway accompanied by a swishing sound. Sure I was imagining things, I turned off the hairdryer and peered out of the bathroom to see Pipy running around the house with a plastic grocery bag attached to his middle. As he ran the bag became a parachute, and out of the parachute tumbled chocolate candy, hitting the walls and bouncing everywhere. The sight was too much. I doubled over, howling with laughter, which brought my husband to the scene. By this time the show was over and a very frightened Pipy was hiding behind a chair with the empty bag still wrapped around him.

What apparently happened was that Pipy, who loves the smell of chocolate, decided he wanted a piece of brightly wrapped Christmas chocolates that filled a pretty candy dish I had set out. I had covered the bowl with the grocery bag, hoping he would leave the candy alone. Since the bowl was on the floor empty, I assumed that in trying to uncover the bowl and help himself he managed to dump the entire contents into the bag and off he ran, trying to get away from the bag that was flying behind him.

It has been a short six months since our son died. Each day is just as hard as the day before, but we put our trust in God. We know that He will get us through our grief to a place where we can have pleasant memories of our son. God even thought to give us a cat who is both a source of comfort and laughter at times when we need it the most.

It seems strange to read something written at the six-month point, which I remember thinking then, that time was crawling by at a snail's pace. And now it has been nine years. I would have told you early on that years were impossible, but God has carried us along. So if you happen to be early in your journey, take heart and take my hand, and we will both lean on God for comfort and support.

Every good present and every perfect gift comes from above, from the Father who made the sun, moon, and stars.
James 1:17, GW.

Walking Wounded

For God so loved. John 3:16.

We are the walking wounded, friend. I see your pain, feel it in your words; it is both pulsing and palpable. This is not a path we would have ever chosen, but it is ours to walk. We do it hand in hand, walking with an unseen Guest who knows our grief firsthand. It was God and His Son, Jesus Christ, who agreed to a plan that they would not have chosen either if there had been another way to save mankind from self-destruction in the hands of this world's evil management.

From my years on this journey, I have the "vantage point" of reflection while looking back to remember all the stages and how God has led. You may not factor God in the equation, and that is okay. But if you don't mind, I want to continue this train of thought.

I was born with an empty, emotional backpack waiting to be filled. All negative things were easy to store in my backpack, which grew heavier as I grew older. I got busy raising a family, and therefore, like most of you, held down two jobs. There was always something to push my nose out of joint so in the backpack it would go. Maybe it was a snide remark made by a coworker or boss, and I was afraid if I spoke up, I'd be fired. Maybe it was a smart remark from one of my children as he skidded out of the driveway, making sure he stayed away until he thought it was safe to return ... and I'd have forgotten. I have a memory like an elephant ... for pain that is. So in the backpack it goes. There's always room for more pain in there. Sound familiar?

And then the unspeakable happened. Suddenly, tragically, we lost our firstborn child to suicide. That pain would not fit in my backpack. It was the size of Mt. Everest and it broke me. I shattered like shards of glass, splintering in all directions. There was nothing left to salvage. The "me" I knew and those around me knew, was no more. It seemed as if time should stand still now, and the atmosphere void of oxygen with not even a heart left to beat.

Perhaps you would describe your experience differently, or maybe you are nodding in agreement. You could add more sentences, and we would all nod in agreement, for many of us are familiar with the trauma of sudden death. It sucks the life out of the living, making even thinking about living seem impossible ... for a time.

But I do have good news. God can recreate. It's His specialty. He loves His sons and daughters on earth with an unconditional love—a love so awesome He watched His own Son be murdered by our ancestors. He loves us still; both Father and Son love us inside and out. They know the trauma we live firsthand. They suffer with us in our grief.

"Spiritual warfare against the world, the flesh, and the devil is one long, continuous struggle. The battleground has front lines and rear flanks. There are soldiers of Christ and backsliders gone AWOL. The Enemy has a strategy, and he's out to kill, maim, and wound. But God's strategy is to advance his kingdom and reclaim enemy territory" (Joni Eareckson Tada, *Diamonds in the Dust* [Grand Rapids, MI: Zondervan Publishing House, 1993]).

God is fighting for us, and Satan is fighting against us, and we are caught in the crossfire in this battle between good and evil. There are converts on both sides. You and I have met both.

Perhaps in your grief you have met those who don't give you the time of day. In their ignorance, they are allowing the enemy to speak through their mouths and work through their actions. If this is more than you can comfortably swallow, that's okay. What I am suggesting is that the picture of spiritual warfare is much larger than our minds can fathom. The whole world groans with the actions of the enemy, and God misses none of it. He hurts when the enemy destroys a child, any child. And too often it is our child. Bear in mind, God is not the destroyer—Satan is (John 10:10).

So where is the good news? This is how I describe it. God is recreating me brick by brick: bricks of hope, forgiveness, love, trust, to name a few. I don't know when I will be completed; perhaps I am a work in progress until Jesus returns. But now I know where to turn. I turn to God. I take off my heavy backpack and drop it at His feet with words that go something like this: "Jesus, please take it. I'm done carrying it." This is an act of complete surrender to a Power greater than I, who sees time from beginning to end, and "giving up" is giving Him permission to act in my life. Surrender must be practiced daily, for it is too easy to get behind the wheel and take over again. And even though my heart is often very heavy, my steps are light and my mind can sing His praises because I know I don't have to fix what I am incapable of. That's His job and He does it with love.

"I'm a Child of the King"

My Father is rich in houses and lands,
He holdeth the wealth of the world in His hands!

Of rubies and diamonds, of silver and gold,
His coffers are full, He has riches untold.

Yes, this is an old, old song, and for some of you younger folk, it may cause you to smile at the old language, but to me it is beautiful and priceless and provides a treasure trove of memories.

You see, my mother taught me this song when I was "knee high to a grasshopper" as they say where I come from. And I can still see us standing around the piano singing as the evening shadows deepened, replacing the last rays of the setting sun.

My Father's own Son, the Savior of men,
Once wandered on earth as the poorest of them;

But now He is pleading our pardon on high,
That we may be His when He comes by and by.

These memories are more precious to me now since my parents have both gone to their rest. Just when they got all of us kids raised and they had the time to relax and enjoy life, maybe even travel a bit, Mother grew sick with Alzheimer's disease. My parents had made a pact between them that they would take care of each other rather than resort to nursing home care. In their eyes it was not an option, and Daddy learned how to take care of Mother. He took over the household duties. He tied her shoelaces and brushed her teeth and combed her hair. He bathed and fed her when she could no longer hold a spoon.

I once was an outcast stranger on earth,
A sinner by choice, an alien by birth,

But I've been adopted, my name's written down,
An heir to a mansion, a robe and a crown.

Those of you who have experience with this hideous disease know that it robs the senses, sometimes slowly, but often quickly. It got a quick grip on Mother, and soon she lost her ability to speak. Unable to say what was on her heart, it frustrated her so, which pained us all as we watched her struggle. But when the family got together once again and stood around the piano, my mother "found her voice."

We were all shocked and hushed to a whisper—transfixed by Mother's beautiful soprano and perfect diction. Her eyes closed, she sang from deep within her soul the words committed to memory so long ago. Apparently what was in her mind and heart from a lifetime of singing returned to gift us all. Her face took on the glow of heaven while she sang—she was free for a few moments. Once the music stopped, the disease gripped Mother's vocal cords and silenced her once again.

A tent or a cottage, why should I care?
They're building a palace for me over there;

Though exiled from home, yet still may I sing:
All glory to God, I'm a child of the King.

Little did I know that while I was learning these words, which meant little to my childish heart, they would come back to me now and bless me once again. Memories may be all we have now, but not for long. We have the hope of the resurrection morning when my mother will sing again. The words of this song remind me of who I am and who I belong to. I long for Jesus' soon return when He will come back and claim His kids and we will be reunited with our loved ones, forever children of the heavenly King.

I'm a child of the King,
A child of the King:
With Jesus my Savior,
I'm a child of the King.

In 1877 Harriet E. Buell wrote the words for this hymn and John B. Sumner composed the music.

Mum Reminders

Time passes. It always amazes me how it does, but should it? When summer days ease into cool nights and the bright, showy colors of fall appear, I am once again reminded that another year has passed. Today was the perfect day to buy an end-of-summer-sale mum. The pickings were slim at the roadside stand, but I found a pretty one that reminds me of daisies. It is large and full with sunny yellow centers surrounded by white petals. Today is a pretty day, and it will look nice where I put it, but no one will notice. He won't see it either, and it won't last long. Like everything else in life it will soon die as frost nibbles at its petals.

Today I will set this mum on my son's grave. I did the same thing eight years ago when I set out a yellow mum under a canopy of blue. Today I plopped down on the lush green grass and stared at the immense blue above me. How could time pass? At first after he died, it seemed like time stood still—as well it should! I felt like everything should come to a screeching halt, shouldn't it? There should be no rushing, noisy traffic, no hustle and bustle of business. Life should stop for everyone in respect for my loss, but it didn't work that way. Time passes, even if slowly, but it does pass. Life continues to move us along as if we are standing on a moving walkway at the airport and forced to keep up with other travelers whether we like it or not.

I couldn't lie on the grass too long or I wouldn't be able to get up (okay, no comments). Groaning as I did so, I remembered that eight years ago I had taken a walk after I had placed the yellow mum on my son's grave. It was a beautiful fall day just like today. I couldn't help but talk in my heart to my son, telling him about all the beauty he was missing. But his heart had been too broken for joy. It was his decision, and his actions have forced me to live with the result. He is unaware of the passage of time or the pain inflicted on his family. He is at peace. I'd rather he be sleeping in his bed where I could wake him up, but I can't. Where he is, I can't call. All contact has been cut off. The wires are severed. There is no communication from my loved ones who have been laid to rest. Not yet anyway.

But soon that will change. God says in His Word that Jesus will return! He will come in the clouds and turn our mourning into dancing! We will shed tears of joy at the glad reunion in the beautiful, immense sky above. Instead of the jarring noise of traffic, heaven's choir will burst into song, and we will forever be with our loved ones where even mums won't die.

You have changed my sobbing into dancing. Psalm 30:11, GW.

He will wipe every tear from their eyes. There won't be any more death. There won't be any grief, crying, or pain, because the first things have disappeared. Revelation 21:4, GW.

Look! He is coming in the clouds. Every eye will see him. Revelation 1:7, GW.

Choose Compassion

Do you remember the oft-repeated children's rhyme, "Sticks and stones will break my bones, but words will never harm me"? Whether hurtful words are said to adults or to children, they cause harm, do they not?

Abraham Lincoln had this to say: "Better to remain silent and be thought a fool than to speak out and remove all doubt." We adults know what this means. How often are we guilty? Is it possible to cast a stone with words? What about facial expressions? How about attitudes?

Have you ever met people who seem to lack a brain filter? A river of opinions may flow unchecked from their mouths, making what President Lincoln said a truth. If I were to ask you the number of times someone has said something hurtful to you in the past year, would you require another hand or two to add up the incidents? Likely you remember the hurtful words. It's sad, heartless, and often downright cruel the things people say, particularly to those who are suffering deeply. Rather than speaking words of compassion, they wax long in their limited understanding of the burdens you carry. They have zero experience but an abundance of "knowledge" picked up from here and there, and sad to say, they are often members of our inner circle. If you have firsthand experience with this type of hurt, I am sorry for your pain.

Words, like throwing stones to drive home a point, leave bruises that last a lifetime. It reminds me of a Bible story that you may recall. Perhaps there are similarities between stones thrown then and "words of stone" that are "thrown" nowadays?

This story is about a single woman named Mary. Pardon my loose translation of the Bible story, which in the telling goes something like this. Mary worked the late shift in the city. She walked the lonely streets at night looking for opportunities to sell her body to make a living. Men liked her good looks but secretly despised her and treated her accordingly. She preferred the wealthier men because they paid her promptly. She performed their preferences and was rewarded for it, but the job had lost its luster. No doubt she was still a beauty in spite of the rough treatment she had to endure in her line of work. But she was tired of the harsh treatment … and the shame. Many a time she was kicked out on the street to spend the rest of the night curled up in a dark alley until the first rays of dawn erased the dark shadows of night, which Mary wished would also erase the ugly memories in her mind.

Mary grew up in the village of Bethany, a suburb of Jerusalem. Often while leaning against the lamppost or curled up in an alley, memories of home flooded her mind. There were always hot meals and a warm bed. She knew her sister Martha and her brother Lazarus would take her back—her room was kept just as she had left it—but they would expect her to give up her lucrative job on the streets in order to live with them. Of course, but who would hire her with her sullied reputation? She had no acceptable work history to speak of. A prospective boss's scoffing would only deepen her shame. As bad as her profession was, she was not ready to call it quits. Not yet.

Then Jesus came to town. He had no home of His own and often stayed with Martha and Lazarus in Bethany. They quickly bonded into a beautiful friendship, and He was always welcome. Jesus was often weary of all the traveling, and Martha always had warm bread from the oven and hot soup simmering in the kettle when she heard

He was on His way. They had good talks too. Lazarus and Martha were eager to learn about God, believing Jesus was God's Son. They poured out their pain about Mary; they worried about her safety and the gossip from the neighborhood. It followed them wherever they went, but they loved their sister and wanted a better life for her.

Back in the city, Mary had a bad night. The trick turned ugly. The man had beaten her after having his way with her. As much as she didn't want to drag her family into her world, she needed them now more than ever, so pulling her veil over her face to hide the bruises, she caught a ride with a passing stranger to Bethany. Martha washed off the dried blood and applied ointment and bandages. Lazarus fretted over her employment while she filled her stomach with the best meal she had eaten in a while, and Jesus just listened.

When she felt safe enough to let her guard down, daring to trust this kind stranger, Jesus began to share with her the love He brought with Him from heaven. He instantly loved Mary as was His nature. His Father loved her too. They talked and talked. Mary felt safe, something she had not felt with any man other than her brother. The Holy Spirit was working on her heart, drawing her to God, and she found her soul satisfied with Jesus' words of hope and healing. Her heart was touched. She had never felt more sinful than she felt at the feet of Jesus, and yet she knew He loved her inside and out. She felt no shame in the presence of Jesus, who knew no sin. But He did not condemn her. Instead, He cast out the demons that haunted her very existence. Her sin was gone!

Mary had found a new love. But after a time, the lure of the bustling city streets pulled at her again. The money was good, and she needed to support herself and think of her future, so she returned to the night life in the big city with deep pockets. It was during one of Mary's business transactions that she was caught in the very act of adultery. Suddenly she was surrounded by men in colorful robes with matching turbans who swiftly drug her half-naked body out into the street. The bright morning sun temporarily blinded her. Try as she might she had little clothing with which to cover her shame. These haughty businessmen in their freshly pressed attire—some she recognized from previous engagements—were hell-bent on making an example of her.

Shielding her eyes against the morning rays, she felt a Presence. Sandaled feet joined her in the circle formed by these blood-thirsty men intent on making a spectacle of her. She knew the law. They intended to spill her blood today. But they wanted to "kill two birds with one stone." Truth be told, they weren't really after her; they were after Jesus. She was the pawn. He was the target. A trap had been set, and they were prepared. Each Pharisee tensely fingered the rough stone he held hidden in the folds of his robe. Each stone would inflict serious damage when heaved at the trembling form. A few blows would forever silence the woman huddled before them, but they craved silencing the Man in the middle more. Much more.

These pious church leaders were hoping to trick Jesus. They hated Him and His followers. He made their blood boil when He preached loving messages of freedom to the people. They wanted control over everyone, and this woman at their feet was to be an example of their supreme authority. There would be one less prostitute when they got through with her. Never mind they had used her. There would be others they'd willingly pay for favors in the dead of night, but today, catching Jesus in His own words would be worth it.

"Hey, Teacher," they yelled. "We caught this woman turning tricks; we caught her in the very act. Moses said we are to stone her to death. What do You say?"

The air echoed with their curt words and then silence fell. It got eerily quiet. Was Jesus going to say anything? Mary barely lifted her mop of sweaty curls to see the sandal-clad feet in front of her. She wanted to cover her head with her arms as if to shield herself against the stones she expected to be hurled at any moment. Still silence. Daring to peek, Mary noticed something strange going on. Jesus was bent over and writing in the soft dirt.

He stood up and said in a quiet, even tone, "Any of you who has never sinned, go ahead and throw your stones at her." Then He returned to His writing. One by one, Mary heard thuds and the shuffling of feet as stones hit the ground and the men slunk away.

It grew quiet again. Only Jesus remained.

Mary did not know what to think. Not only was she a nearly-naked mess, but she had been trembling with the expectation of death. Now all she wanted to do was get to her feet and unabashedly throw her arms around her Savior. Jesus reached down and took her hands, pulling her to her feet. All the feelings of guilt and shame vanished in an instant as He said to her, "[Mary], neither do I say you are guilty. Go on your way and do not sin again" (John 8:11, NLV).

Perhaps you can see the correlation between the stones of this ancient story and the stony behavior of people today; people who liberally condemn the behavior of others with their stony words, piercing the hearts of those who hear them. Self-righteous folks form circles around hurting families. They set ultimatums. They may draw a circle in the sand with you and Jesus in the middle. They throw stones. They have their say. They share their personal truth through stinging words. Then they wait for Jesus to finish you off. After all, if He is who He says He is, God tolerates no sin. Someone has sinned and must be punished. Even though surviving families will bear the crushing pain of loss for the rest of their natural lives, they expect Jesus to not only agree with them, but pronounce final judgment on you or your loved ones right here, right now, just as they have done. They know the law and it has been broken.

But how did Jesus treat Mary? She was set free by the One who would later die for all sins: past, present, and future. He was her Savior, and she fell deeply in love with Him at that moment. Though the world was harsh and sinful and people made it clear that she was worth nothing, Jesus accepted her as she was, forgave her sins, and set her free. He treats us the same, does He not?

Therefore if the Son makes you free, you shall be free indeed.
John 8:36, NKJV.

Life Is Like Salad

If you search for salad recipes on the Internet, you will find that the choices are limitless. And so are the dressings and toppings. If you go to a restaurant, there are plenty of options to tempt any palette. Do you have a favorite? My oldest son did. His all time hands down favorite was Three Bean Salad. If I knew he was planning a visit home, I'd be sure to mix it up well in advance to marinate and chill so it would have the perfect blend of flavors. When he arrived home, I would watch him enjoy it, savoring each bite.

In some ways, tossing a salad is like life. There is a little "lettuce alone," some bitter "memory" herbs, "teary-eyed" onions, croutons for the hard experiences we face, plenty of color in our veggie choices to brighten up the day, and a little squeeze of lemony tartness to balance the flavors in our memory banks. Indeed, our lives are a mix of joy, sadness, and everything in between.

As with a salad we are as simple as we are complex; as interesting as we are plain. In my ministry, which God and I do together, He sends people to cross my path who have also known loss, and we grieve together. It's not all sadness or it could become unbearable, but it is a mixture of all that we find in our lives. We face each day with broken-but-mending hearts because of who He says He is. God gives us the strength to go on no matter what our circumstances are.

Like Three Bean Salad, the colors, textures, and flavors of our life experiences mix together and marinate as we live each day in the strength of Jesus and the companionship of one another.

And how blessed all those in whom you live, whose lives become roads you travel; They wind through lonesome valleys, come upon brooks, discover cool springs and pools brimming with rain! God-traveled, these roads curve up the mountain, and at the last turn—Zion! God in full view! Psalm 84:5–7, MSG.

Peace Be Still

A violent windstorm popped up out of nowhere. Towering, foaming waves bashed the fishing boat and drenched the men aboard. It was a violent storm, unlike anything they had encountered while out at sea. It must have frightened them to think that this storm could be the one they had always feared. This trip could be their last. Frantically, these burly fishermen bailed to no avail. Clearly the boat was sinking. Obviously they were no match for nature's fury.

But this was no ordinary storm. And this was no ordinary group of men. One of them was the Son of God, and He was fast asleep in the back of the boat, totally unconcerned for their safety, or so it seemed to the disciples.

So they woke him up and said to him, "Teacher, don't you care that we're going to die?"

Then he got up, ordered the wind to stop, and said to the sea, "Be still, absolutely still!" The wind stopped blowing, and the sea became very calm.

He asked them, "Why are you such cowards [timid and fearful]? Don't you have any faith yet?"

They were overcome with fear and asked each other,

"Who is this man? Even the wind and the sea obey him!" (Mark 4:37–41, GW).

Is this not our question most days?

Master, don't you care if we perish? We call out for Him in the night when we can't fall asleep, and we call out to Him in the day when we are reminded of our needs. Does He answer? Is He listening? The disciples had Jesus in the boat with them, and yet they tried to save themselves. The Creator of all things, the Savior of the world, was taking a nap in the boat. He was that close when the wind shifted, caught the sails, and was about to capsize their vessel.

When they finally remembered who was on board with them, they asked Him, "Do you care?"

Does He? Is there evidence in the following verse that He cares? What does it say to your heart? "When calamity overtakes you like a storm, when disaster engulfs you like a cyclone, and anguish and distress overwhelm you … all who listen to me will live in peace" (Proverbs 1:27, 33, NLT).

He was in the boat then, and He is near you and me now—always loving, always wooing, always longing for a personal relationship. So He knocks on the door of our hearts. We can choose to let Him in. We can choose to start a friendship. We can choose to surrender our worries, to stop bailing on our own. We can choose to simply ask the Redeemer to guide us to a place of safety when storms in our lives arise.

I have told you these things so you may have peace in Me. In the world you will have much trouble. But take hope! I have power over the world! John 16:33, NLV.

And the Oscar Goes to . . .

Please, don't misunderstand. I have nothing against bestowing praise on our fellow human beings for a job well done. But this story is aimed at our spiritual eyesight where we may not be so inclined to look. As Paul quoted Jeremiah, "Whoever wants to boast must boast of what the Lord has done" (1 Corinthians 1:31, GNT).

What do you think he is talking about? I believe the best way to achieve personal understanding is to read what Paul says in 1 Corinthians and compare it with a variety of other texts, allowing Scripture to speak for itself. And if you don't mind, may I share a personal story in an attempt to illustrate Paul's point?

If you are a woman, you understand the desire to wear make-up some days or every day in an attempt to cover up. There are days when one wanders slowly through the makeup aisles hoping for a new idea. One particular day as I was wandering through the department store, I was ready to be approached and challenged with a new idea, actually a new cover up. Mine needed sprucing up. Could they help?

The sweet young thing behind the counter was energetic and delightful, the perfect sales person. She pointed to a chair, and I sat down, ready and willing to be made over into a more youthful form of myself. Tall order, I know. But why not aim high? Apparently that was exactly her thinking, but I was floored when a few minutes later she handed me the mirror and with a flourish asked, "How do you like it?"

I was speechless ... flabbergasted actually. I needed sunglasses to shield me from the glare as I looked at the face staring back at me from the mirror. I pondered what words could safely be said in this eager young thing's presence. She waited ... and waited. What could I say? I looked like I was bound for Mardi Gras! I had bright blue shimmer raccoon-eye shades that covered me from side to side. Yes, I exaggerate for effect, but it was blue, no doubt about that. And I wasn't headed for New Orleans—I was headed to a wedding. Tamer, elegant, understated was the look I was aiming for. No doubt I had failed to communicate my desires to the sweet girl behind the counter!

I had stalled long enough. "No, I don't like it," I answered softly. It seemed the only thing I could truthfully say. She was crestfallen. She pouted, "You mean *you* don't like it?" She was obviously taking it personally. I tried again to explain the look I was going for. She was not listening. Her countenance stated a determined attitude as she looked about for a guinea pig. She found one. Her eyes lit on a fellow employee who approached her work space obviously looking for something for a customer. She stopped him in his tracks and asked him what he thought. I wanted to bolt, but they blocked the exit. I wanted to slide out of the chair, but that seemed too ridiculous a notion for someone with gray in her hair, so I waited. He stared. He walked around me, chin in hand, apparently looking for a better angle. Oh, dear. This was entirely more than I had bargained for.

Finally he spoke, drawing back as if great distance would give him better perspective, "I think it looks ... great!" He had taken too long. Like me, he didn't want to hurt the sweet girl's feelings. But the makeup artist was on a roll and picking up speed. She was determined to find someone, anyone, who would give her glowing makeup job glowing praise. Okay. Sigh. This was quickly becoming an unforgettable experience.

Then I heard her "yell." "Hey, could you come here a minute?" No. She didn't. Oh, but she did. She waved someone down who was innocently walking by, obviously not shopping for makeup. I turned around to see whom she had captured and saw the face of a bewildered senior not unlike myself. I can't find the right word for the expression she wore, only to say that the sweet young thing was not going to get the A+ she desired. The lady hemmed and hawed and delayed to the point of further humiliation for me and exasperation for the clerk. "You mean you *don't* like it?" Her words seemed to echo across the entire store.

"Well," the genteel lady spoke finally, "it isn't quite my taste." Quickly she escaped. There was a lull. Now it was my turn to put space between the sweet clerk and me. Yes, there were stares as I hurried to the door. But I realized that I was quite content with my own face. I could leave the makeup shopping to other customers.

Perhaps this story does not illustrate Paul's point, or maybe it does. The sales clerk was more interested in seeking praise for herself than she was seeking to please the customer.

Remember what the King of kings did for His disciples? He lowered Himself to a kneeling position and washed their dusty feet. He took on the role of a servant and washed the disciples' dirty, grimy feet—the lowest part of the body and the part most easily contaminated with the dirt of life. But He took advantage of the opportunity to teach His disciples by example how to experience and share humility.

We are not given to humility. We are born with a spirit of pride. We seek the praise of others. We glory in ourselves. It is fine to take pride in a job well done, and we lavish praise on our children with the intent of stimulating them to do their best. I am not suggesting that we change these habits, but I am suggesting that we all look deeper into what God would want us to do. And then follow His example.

Glorify your name, not ours, O Lord! Cause everyone to praise your loving-kindness and your truth. Psalm 115:1, TLB.

A Perfect Pear

Our son's wedding was beautiful in every possible way—even with the sound of gentle rain falling on a canopy of leafy green. He and his lovely bride spoke their vows to each other, enveloped by a giant old tree, which seemed to clasp them in a mighty embrace. Precious words, precious smiles, precious tender moments for them to hold forever in their hearts, and we too will remember forever as we share their joy. I am filled with happiness that my son married the woman he treasures, the one he will treasure for the rest of his life. She is lovely in every way, and we now have a daughter added to our family to love.

When you lose someone to death, you have to figure out how to live with it and go on, in spite of missing them. It's difficult, isn't it? Do you fake a smile at happy occasions, or do you truly embrace the moments of happiness that may be around every corner as you move along with life? I say, let's choose to embrace them. Let's pour ourselves into each and every moment as God gives us breath and grace.

I have promised to tell the truth, so I admit that I wondered if I could bear the happiness of our son's wedding without feeling sadness too. My son would marry without sharing his special day with his brother, who would likely have been his best man. Instead, he was blessed to have as his best man a friend who is like a brother. In fact, all three boys grew up together. My son could not have made a wiser choice, and surprisingly, it brought me no pain.

I had time to process both the bitter and sweet emotions during the engagement period, and I promised myself, with God's help, to shed no tears of sadness, and my prayers were answered. With the falling rain my attire and hairdo, like everyone else's, got dampened, but my heart overflowed with joy. Actually we prayed that the dark clouds would move elsewhere, and since they didn't, perhaps the raindrops were symbolic of God's tears of joy.

There were a few moments of painful conflict that came quite unexpectedly. As the newlyweds held each other and danced and swayed to an old favorite, "Love Me Tender" by Elvis Presley, the beauty of the moment put me in overload, and tears began to trickle down my cheeks. A friend handed me a tissue and soothingly rubbed my back. I didn't have an explanation for the tears. But I didn't apologize for them either. It was a moment of extreme pleasure combined with reminders of days gone by ... the old song ... my sons all grown up ... one laid to rest ... the other one expressing pure joy with every look and movement. So I let some tears fall. He did not see them, for he only had eyes for his beautiful bride.

The lovely couple chose as their wedding theme "Pick a Perfect Pear." To celebrate their cute idea, we munched salad greens with fresh pear slices, enjoyed delectable pear dumplings, sipped pear cider with each toast, and took away fresh pears to enjoy later. From the first glance to the last photo, our son and his bride had put their love for each other into every frame.

Thank You, God, for preparing and pairing these darling children to be a "pear" of beauties for the rest of their days on earth. Thank You for giving Your blessing. What more could we ask for?

The Touch of Leather

Jesus reached out his hand and touched the man. Matthew 8:3.

Stuff represents life. Perhaps you, too, place value on things that once belonged to a loved one you have been forced to say goodbye to. Maybe you decorated the mantel or the shelves in a curio cabinet with their things. Or maybe you keep their room just as they left it. It matters. Their stuff matters. For me, one of the things I cherish from my son is his billfold because it represents his life.

I am drawn to leather—good quality leather—with its rich aroma and smooth touch. Lest this sound like a description of a leather skirt or pants, let me hasten to add that I would never wear leather on any place other than my feet, but I love leather purses, leather Bibles, leather car seats … and my son's leather billfold.

It's just a thing. And not a very big thing, but it holds notes, a little money, and his identity. Other than our photos, it is all that remains to remind me that my firstborn once had a life.

Just like mail. Does anyone get excited about getting mail? Remember *You've Got Mail*, the movie with Tom Hanks and Meg Ryan? Both could hardly wait to get home, hit the power button, and wait for the computer to warm up to hear the magical words, "you've got mail!" Be it the rarity of snail mail or the frequency of tweets and texts, who does not relish the exchange of words with those we care about?

Mail, like my son's billfold, contains words that imply life. He once had a very busy, fulfilling, successful life—or so we thought. He had an address where he got mail. After his death, all future mail was transferred to us and still it comes. The latest is a Subaru car sales advertisement—advertising their product, encouraging him to "come in and take a test-drive in the all-new 2014 Subaru Forester 2.OXT with a 250hp turbocharged Subaru Boxer engine."

Of course they have no idea that he is no longer on earth's radar screen, but for his mom it is a painful reminder that he is not here. I wish he were here to take a test drive and tell us all about the new Subaru or to share his excitement over changes in his life in pursuit of his dreams. But it's not so.

In our grief journey when we are able to process our child's life, we realize that with hindsight comes clarity. But we are unable to see the future. If we were, we would have done everything in our power to keep our loved one—who has passed away—safe. If I had had a little foresight, I would have realized the amount of pain my son was carrying. Depression leads to bleakness and frantic darkness and excruciating pain of mind and heart. I can't begin to comprehend what he went through before he made the decision that changed our lives forever.

Right now I have so many questions without answers. However, my questions will get answered one day and so will yours. God has promised to wipe away all our tears, which suggests to me that He will reach out and touch our faces and wrap us in a hug. There will be conversation and explanations too, don't you think? Perhaps when I see my son's face with his cute grin and little chuckle, I will forget I ever had questions. But for now all I have is a billfold to remind me of the years I had his sweet presence in my life. I would gladly trade a piece of leather for the touch of his hand ... soon, may it be very soon.

He will wipe away all tears from their eyes, and there shall be no more death, nor sorrow, nor crying, nor pain. All of that has gone forever. Revelation 21:4, TLB.

Silent Salute

There is something powerful in our military salute, and I love it! I love my country. I am sure you do too, and we support everyone who defends our freedom. It is a costly task, leaving spouses, children, parents, siblings, and other family and friends to mourn. Thankfully, there are men and women who are committed to defending the United States of America and keeping our country free—may we always be free.

One of my children served in the U.S. Air Force, and I am proud of his accomplishments. He served his country faithfully, doing his best, giving his all. Fortunately, he lives to share his stories.

Recently I listened to our President as he shared heroic stories about our fallen comrades, those who gave themselves as a living sacrifice to defend our homeland. I know the pain in the hearts of the families will never go away. We owe them a debt of gratitude, and our president paid the nation's respect in their honor; he recounted their stories, handed out medals to those who were fortunate to have survived, and gave them each a crisp salute.

Perhaps this story will seem disjointed. For that I apologize. The pain in my mind and heart slow down the flow of words to the page. My mind swirls in search of just the right words in an attempt to convey feelings from my heart to yours. Perhaps you understand this internal conflict? Those of us on a survival journey "get it" and require no further explanation. I have a point. Really. The point is about the salute.

The images are forever stuck in my mind. We had gathered to say our last goodbye to my firstborn son. We were sitting in the shade under the canopy that hot day. I remember sunshine, but I don't remember what time of day it was. Apparently it didn't make the cut in my memory. You know the drill. Most of us have experienced such a gathering at least once in our lives and too many times it is in honor of one of our children ... way too often. If you, too, have lost a child, let me say how sorry I am for your pain.

My stepson had spent much of his life serving his country. He looked fine in his uniform, creased and pressed to perfection. He had the gait, the language, the perfect performance, and the manners. He knew how to salute and had done so often when in the presence of a senior officer. Nothing less would be tolerated. It is a habit, but respectful to be sure.

Now, back to the tent. The last words of comfort had been said, although I don't remember them. I heard sound—mostly my own weeping. We each caressed the box ... oh how I hate the box ... but it contained precious remains so I must cherish it. Slowly we stood to our feet. It was time to leave the box behind, for that was the decision we made. Mind-numbing pain equals mind-numbing decisions, which could later be mulled over and regretted, but not now. Now we had to bid a fond farewell to the box displayed on red velvet. No matter the softness of fabric ... nothing about this moment softens the blows to my heart.

And then I saw it. My stepson stood to his feet and approached the stand where the box rested. He paused, then snapped to attention, clicking his heels together, and gave his brother a sharp salute. Silence. Even the air seemed to stand still in respect. Through blurry eyes I witnessed a shower of honor bestowed on my firstborn by his step-brother. For him, the salute offered the highest respect, love, and praise to his fallen brother. No, my boy did not die in combat, not like we usually think of combat. And yet it *is* combat. The forces of evil are fighting against the forces of good. My heavenly Father, in His unfathomable love and mercy, gently allowed a hurting heart to rest ... for now.

Slowing the story down frame by frame is not intended to draw tears (even though mine flow) but to bring relief. If you are a parent who has lost a child or you lost your sibling or a dear friend, you understand the need to slow it down, do you not? The heart aches to unearth pain. The heart aches to release to the wind the agony it feels. The heart aches to share it, for it is in the sharing that we deepen our understanding of loss where mind and heart ache to be connected again. We can't bring our loved one back, but we can open our hearts for the benefit of others who may not have experienced such tragedy. Not to be morbid, but somehow in the telling of our stories, we help others to become wiser, more reflective, and more understanding in the love and honor we feel about our fallen child. Does that make sense?

Like a maze we work our way through twists, turns, stops, and starts. We tackle the pain from within, trying to put into words what we feel, not only for the healing of our hearts, but to help those who cannot fathom our suffering. With encouragement from a willing listener, we are able to unearth some painful words deep in the core of our being and release them for a bit of relief. Granted the process repeats often, for there is always more, still more. Such is the process of healing, slow and steady.

For I can do everything God asks me to with the help of Christ who gives me the strength and power. Philippians 4:13, TLB.

Purity of Mama Pain

You've kept track of my every toss and turn through the sleepless nights, each tear entered in your ledger, each ache written in your book. Psalm 56:8, MSG

Perhaps this title gives you "word whiplash," a double take as it were. That's okay. The title looks a bit strange on paper to me too, but I want to write about mothers losing their children to suicide, which you may not have interest in. If you stop reading here, you won't hurt my feelings. Since there is one suicide death every sixty-six minutes—actually ninety-nine suicide deaths every sixty-six minutes around the globe—I think the topic is worthy of the time it takes to write about and yours to read. Most of us know at least one family who has lost someone they love to suicide. Unless a mother precedes her child in death, she will outlive her child, surviving the aftermath of terrible loss. I know this grief first hand, so I hope you will give me a little wiggle room with my choice of words. They are intended to bless us both.

If you are not a mother but you lost someone you loved to suicide, I can speak around your pain and perhaps there are many similarities, but I cannot speak from personal experience to your grief.

A mama's grief is unique. It is this one I know and have known for nine years. It's not an easy journey as you may know. It is a tough assignment, and it certainly takes more than it gives, but there is gain in the giving back to help others along the same journey. This is what I do. In writing, I picture myself dropping back to link arms with you as we walk and share together. Hugs are exchanged. Tissues given. And in the sharing, our loads are lifted temporarily. I hope you have experienced this, for no one need walk alone. There are many grief support groups out there and many as close as a click on your computer. If you aren't familiar with the grief sites on social media, perhaps you will look for them. I was astounded to see the number of people, mostly women and mostly mothers, so if you are a mother you will be in comfortable company of those who "get it."

May I speak frankly? Suicide is a word fraught with drama. As I have written before, it is often used in circles where it does not belong, especially in the media as an attention-grabbing word. From sportswriters to newscasters, they all use it, and I have had to learn to accept it. What else can be done?

But what of those closer to us: family, friends, and coworkers. Is there drama around suicide there too? I say "yes" because that is my experience. Funerals and weddings seem to bring out not only the best but also the worst in human behavior. My memories of our memorial service are murky with the actions of others around me totally out of place and unacceptable, but I was powerless to stop it or change it at the time, so I must live with the memories of it. But there is something I *can* do. I can speak openly in the hope that it will strike a resounding chord in some of you who will share it with others for maximum exposure.

I'd like to share my thoughts about funeral drama. Every family is different. Perhaps yours surrounded you and continues to support you in various ways. Trust me, it's a blessing when they do. But some of us cannot think about the loss of our child without seeing the faces of those who tried to steal the day for their own purposes, therefore:

- I have given myself permission to move them out of my memory surrounding my child's death.

- They are excluded from any thought I have about my child going forward.

- I choose to honor my child's memory by keeping my grief pure with his name engraved on it. My tears have given me clarity over time. I will continue to shed tears as will you. I choose to think of them as pure as raindrops, glistening rainbow colors in the sunlight with prismlike beauty. His memory deserves care, and I will give it most tenderly.

I know others miss him and grieve in their own way. Bless them! I am glad they honor my son too, but they are outside the circle of my heart. Within me is the heart of a mother designed by the Creator with huge tear ducts! We can cry at a whim. We fall asleep drenched in tears, do we not? Each breathing moment our minds struggle to think about anything or anyone else, especially in the beginning when grief is raw and bleeding. If you desire to move certain faces out of your memory, then do it. No one else need know. No one else around you can understand your mama heart, can they?

There is only One who truly understands. It is He who created us mamas with an enormous capacity to love! It is God, our heavenly Father. He knows all things, so I assume that He alone understands our pain. So I talk to Him about my son all the time. I have no words, but I ask Him to write through me. If you are touched deep in your heart at what is shared here, please consider that it is the touch from God's own heart. Our loving God understands mama grief. He loves for us to snuggle up to Him, so fear not as you approach. He welcomes us with open arms, and we can stay on His lap as long as we like and return time and time again. He offers His handkerchief to dry our tears and murmurs encouraging words that our hearts understand.

There will come a day when we will cry mama tears for the last time. He has promised to dry our eyes for the last time. There will be no reason for tears of sadness in heaven because there will be no more death! Until that amazing day, we have reason to hope in these beautiful promises.

But the Lord says: Don't cry any longer, for I have heard your prayers and you will see them again; they will come back to you from the distant land of the enemy. Jeremiah 31:16, TLB.

I heard a loud shout from the throne saying, "Look, the home of God is now among men, and he will live with them and they will be his people; yes, God himself will be among them. He will wipe away all tears from their eyes, and there shall be no more death, nor sorrow, nor crying, nor pain. All of that has gone forever." Revelation 21:3, 4, TLB.

Calling All Mothers

I know what day is coming. I have a calendar. But even if I didn't, there is plenty of advertising out there to remind me. I'm going to be honest here and tell you that I'd rather skip over Mother's Day. It's not because I don't have a loving family who shares hugs and cards and gifts with me, because I do, and I love them dearly. But my heart still aches for one more; one whose presence is deeply missed by all of us. This piece is dedicated to all surviving mothers—mothers who are surviving the loss of a child. We may have other children whom we love, but we have outlived one whose absence causes us unspeakable pain.

Perhaps I should spend our time together wisely and search for kernels of truth that will provide more lasting hope than the wonderful, but temporary blessings such as bouquets and cards and invitations to dinner. No, I don't have them on the tip of my tongue, but in the digging, God will be right there to make sure that what we unearth will be just the blessing we both need to hear to get us through this bittersweet holiday.

It is only by God's amazing grace that I got to where I am today. As we moms know, one can never plan ahead for grief. There is no space in the mind to allow for such a thing. Tragedy sucks the air out of our sails immediately after loss. There is no air to breathe, and we'd rather there not be any. We'd rather die after the death of a child than live.

But time has a way of ticking passed when we aren't looking and when we don't think it can. My world crashed on top of me when my son died. This "Humpty Dumpty" had no desire to be put back together again, ever! There was nothing left of who I was. Others wanted me back just the way I had been, but that normal had died. There would have to be a new normal, a re-creation, but I was incapable of re-creating. It was above my "pay grade" so to speak. It would have to be a miracle. Was that possible?

This is where God stepped in. He is making me new once more. In the process, He is making me less shy, less "I can't." He has encouraged me to journal my feelings for His eyes only. I refused at first, but He continued to encourage. I still refused. Back and forth we went until I gave in. Staring at a blank computer screen, I wondered *where are the words going to come from?* But once the dam broke, it unleashed a torrent of deep pain that eventually became a book, *Shattered by Suicide, My Conversations With God After the Tragic Death of My Son.* Who knew this was possible? Not me. Only God knew. Only God sees the bigger picture. Only He can see what we can become in His strength.

Together, you and I walk this grief journey arm in arm. Unfortunately, new ones join us every day, for the gush of loss continues. Each day we are reminded of our sorrow, but each day we are encouraged, in His strength, to survive and even thrive. Yes, thriving is possible. Hope is possible. And even joy is possible on this impossible journey.

God writes through me. He asked me to be a conduit, to be His hands, feet, and heart to those who follow after. The stats are so high, so tragic. Every forty seconds there is a death by suicide around the globe. I shudder to think of the impact this makes on families everywhere! But all death of children, no matter the cause, takes a heavy toll on parents and siblings and all who love them. All death breaks God's heart too.

I am but a drop in the bucket, but collectively as we are able to pick ourselves up and join the human race again, we make a difference. One drop alone makes little impact, but many drops make a stream, and the stream fills many buckets. It takes time to be able to focus on the blessings that still surround us, but they are there and continue to flow. Like that stream we continue to live by God's amazing grace. We continue to live to be an inspiration to others. God can use each willing "cracked pot," which is what I call myself. I am a cracked pot, broken by circumstances out of my control, but not out of His.

If you have yet to find a Bible text that describes your loss, you may find this one helpful, which I have personalized: "The Lord is close to the brokenhearted [me] and saves those who are crushed in spirit [my son]" (Psalm 34:18).

Be encouraged by the many promises in God's Book. It is my "go to" place when my cracked pot seems to leak faster than it fills. Perhaps these texts will encourage you as they encourage me. It is a place to start, and there are many more where they come from.

To have faith is to be sure of the things we hope for, to be certain of the things we cannot see. Hebrews 11:1, GNT.

This hope is a safe anchor for our souls. It will never move. Hebrews 6:19, NLV.

Back in Nain

Jesus wept. John 11:35.

These two words are familiar to many. We recognize them as the shortest verse in the Bible. It is short, but meaningful. Jesus wept at the tomb of His friend, Lazarus. I wonder why He bothered with tears when He knew that He was about to wake up His friend and restore him to his family? When I picture this scene in my mind, I can't help but wish that my family could be restored. I'm sure you have the same desire, for there are many of us who mourn.

If your heart cries out in longing and screams against the injustice that death brings, you are not alone. I'm with you. I get it. I understand your pain, and I am so sorry for your suffering. Like me, if you have outlived one of your offspring, you know the deep, insatiable pain that has taken up residence in our hearts. We long for life to be put in reverse and take us back to a time when our family was complete, but it doesn't work that way … or did it? The Author of life who brought Lazarus back to life did it again for the widow of Nain. Please read on …

"Jesus went with his disciples to the village of Nain, with the usual great crowd at his heels. A funeral procession was coming out as he approached the village gate" (Luke 7:11, 12, TLB).

Hit the pause button.

In my collection of life experiences, more than once I have stopped while traveling somewhere on any normal day to let a stream of cars out of the driveway of a funeral home. The lead car is always a limo. Each car following behind has a flag fluttering on its antenna. Count the cars. There are many. I let my mind tiptoe … for just a moment … into what it must be like for the grieving family and friends about now, but soon impatience takes over, and I'm eager to be on my way. But let's linger for just a moment longer. What if you were in one of those vehicles? What if you were in the first car right behind the hearse? Many of us have been, and it's awful. It's mind-numbing. You aren't even aware of other cars traveling in the same direction … unless you hear a radio blaring in the next lane, and its jarring bass reminds you that life is running on normal for others. Maybe it's a beautiful sunny day, but you don't notice. Maybe it's raining buckets, but you're unaware that you're getting drenched. Your heart is crushed. Someone you love is taking their final ride to their place of rest, and you want to scream in protest!

Maybe that's how this widow felt. Let's continue the story. . .

"The boy who had died was the only son of his widowed mother, and many mourners from the village were with her. When the Lord saw her, his heart overflowed with sympathy" (verses 12, 13).

Hit the pause button again.

Perhaps you understand what this mother was feeling? Perhaps you've been there … but she had the advantage, although she didn't know it yet. Her heart was broken. Her eyes were so full of tears she could hardly make out the face of the Man standing right beside her. Let's read on.

"'Don't cry!' he said. Then he walked over to the coffin and touched it, and the bearers stopped. 'Laddie,' he said, 'come back to life again.'

"Then the boy sat up and began to talk to those around him! And Jesus gave him back to his mother" (verses 13–15).

Hit the pause button again.

Sometimes powerful stories such as this one are covered so quickly in just a few sentences that they barely have time to sink into our pores. There had to have been many emotions tumbling over one another in this mother's mind as she stood transfixed, looking into the face of her very-much-alive boy! How could this be? She knew he had died; she had felt his cold, lifeless body. She had agonized over his death and shuddered against the loneliness that would stalk her remaining days ... but he was alive! Can you imagine her joy? Maybe she did cartwheels she was so happy ... or not, but read on.

"A great fear swept the crowd, and they exclaimed with praises to God, 'A mighty prophet has risen among us,' and, 'We have seen the hand of God at work today.'

"The report of what he did that day raced from end to end of Judea and even out across the borders" (verses 16, 17).

God had not forgotten. Oh how I would have loved to trade places! How I would have loved for Jesus to be in my town and stop my funeral procession and wake up my son! But it was her son, her joy. It was Jesus' joy too. Can you picture His face as He watched the two of them embrace? How wonderful to be Jesus and witness joy between two of His created and reunited children. How wonderful to be Jesus with His power over death!

Some may scoff at this story, but I choose to believe that all Bible stories are true, and although they happened a long time ago, they are still fresh today, helping to grow our faith. Jesus healed. He breathed life back into death. In His presence, death had no power, not then or now. But we can't reach out and touch Jesus today, not like people could then. As much as I might have longed for my son's chest to fill with air and for him to sit up in his coffin, it didn't happen. I must wait. I'm impatient, probably like you, but we must wait.

Remember, we won't always be sad. The grief journey is hard and seemingly endless, but it won't always be this way. Just as I believe this story to be true, I also believe that our children will be raised up again with brand new, immortal bodies, and death will be no more. Until then, friend, we hope.

He will swallow up death forever. The Almighty Lord will wipe away tears from every face, and he will remove the disgrace of his people from the whole earth. The Lord has spoken.
Isaiah 25:8, GW.

Through him you believe in God, who raised him from death and gave him glory; and so your faith and hope are fixed on God. 1 Peter 1:21, GNT.

The Crust Caper

A picture speaks a thousand words, don't you agree? If you are a lover of strawberries like me, a picture of a basket of strawberries shouts volumes and beckons me to bake. Strawberry season is one of my favorite times of the year! It makes us strawberry lovers start to drool at the thought of fresh strawberry pie. I had everything on hand. I hadn't done the back-breaking labor of picking my own berries, but I had picked out the best looking berries I could find at the grocery store and grabbed the topping. The crust was easy. I had one in the freezer just begging to be baked, so the stage was set, and yummy thoughts were set in motion.

That evening I baked the crust and formulated my plan. After it cooled, it was going in the fridge overnight while dreams of piled-high strawberries danced in my head. How wonderful to share a thing of beauty with dinner guests the next day. Unfortunately, I forgot to put the crust away before I went to bed. Big mistake! I know the rule. Cats "cat about" while people sleep—our area rugs are always scattered out of place in the morning. I can hear them thunder across the wood floor and slide. I know they stay off the counters while we're watching, but there are no rules at night, and this night had been no exception.

As soon as my feet hit the floor the next morning, I remembered the pie crust. I hastened to the kitchen to see if there was any damage. Yep, there was a mess on the counter and on the floor. A glass dish had been knocked off the counter and had shattered. I grabbed a broom and dust pan to clean up the broken glass, occasionally looking around for a cat with a smile on his face. None seen. The two little ones were too curious and too close at hand to be guilty—so like children. The culprit was probably hiding out somewhere.

We have no hidden cameras in our house, but oh I wish we did. I would have paid good money to see this in action. I can only assume that the culprit was Pipy, who prefers our food to his. He's our usual hijinks cat, and trouble seems to follow him whenever the lights go out at night, so my forgetfulness was his gain.

It was after I cleaned up the shards of glass that I noticed the pie crust. It was cracked on one side and a large chunk missing on the other. I could picture Pipy sitting in the middle of the pie crust trying his best to get more crust in his tummy before the day dawned. I turned around, my eyes zeroing in on his favorite pillow. He'd been sleeping ... yawn ... but with my appearance he was suddenly on high alert, watching for signs of danger. Oh well. Why bother scolding him? He would never connect the caper to my sudden irrational behavior, not that he hadn't seen it before. He looked rather bored actually. *Back to the nap,* his body language seemed to say.

I figured it was too late to activate the five-second rule. So this crust was garbage. We'd have to settle for strawberries and cream for dessert instead. And Pipy would live to see another day with the possibility of more delectable delights.

I am thankful that God doesn't have a five-second rule when I goof up. He is patient, kind, loving, and understanding of my messes. Who else would willingly forgive the second I ask? Gone ... just like that. Now it's my turn to forget and resist the temptation to fish where God has posted a "No Fishing" sign. My sins are buried in the depths, and I am to forget about them just as He already has.

I just love God's forgiveness. Don't you?

You will again have compassion on us. You will overcome our wrongdoing. You will throw all our sins into the deep sea. Micah 7:19, GW.

No Ordinary Tea Party

He [Jesus] got up from the meal, took off his outer clothing, and wrapped a towel around his waist. After that, he poured water into a basin and began to wash his disciples' feet, drying them with the towel that was wrapped around him. He came to Simon Peter, who said to him, "Lord, are you going to wash my feet?" Jesus replied, "You do not realize now what I am doing, but later you will understand." "No," said Peter, "you shall never wash my feet." Jesus answered, "Unless I wash you, you have no part with me." John 13:4-8.

To be completely honest, I have to admit that the conversation between Jesus and Peter regarding the washing of Peter's feet doesn't sound all that bad at first. In fact, it reads like a conversation I might have had with Jesus. Imagine coming to the table sorely in need of a pedicure. Embarrassed? A resounding "yes!" from this corner. The same kind of feelings might run through me if I suddenly found myself in need of emergency medical attention and remembering too late that all my decent underwear was back home in the drawer …

In this story, more than likely I would have been as unprepared as Peter, for this was no ordinary tea party. Let me explain. For months a group of women had been meeting for Bible study and prayer. Over time they became close enough to comfortably share with one another the deep concerns Jesus laid on their hearts. One cannot be in such a group for long without feeling the Holy Spirit's nudging to "get real," and these women responded and bonded in their love for Jesus and each other. But as often happens in life, the group meetings succumbed to hectic schedules, and the women disappeared back into the rat race of living.

But when you have had something so good and so meaningful, how do you let it go? There were heart longings, and one participant took it upon herself to extend an invitation to the other women to come to her home for tea. Sidebar: if I had been the one extending an invitation for tea in my relatively unexplored territory of hospitality, it would likely have just been tea. You know what I mean? You take a mug from the cabinet, heat water in the microwave, toss in a tea bag, and you're done. There might be some thought as to what to serve with it, but nah … just tea and a friend for starters … but never mind the sidebar because I'd be painting the wrong picture in your head, so back to the real story.

Each friend received a personal, handwritten invitation to come over for tea. Perhaps the hostess baked a loaf of pumpkin bread or stopped by the local deli for something delectable. At any rate, she was prepared to serve tea. Since I know few details, I will embellish with a sprinkle of ideas from my imagination to keep it interesting. Let's say she covered the table with a crisp linen tablecloth and washed and dried the delicate china teacups and plates saved for special occasions until they sparkled, and maybe she made a pitcher of lemonade for those who preferred their beverage chilled.

The doorbell chimed. The women arrived one by one. The first lady stepped over the threshold with her hands wrapped around an exquisite vase of fresh blooms for the table. Another came in bearing a lovely tray of warm-out-of-the-oven scones just itching to be filled with strawberry jam from a crystal bowl. A third came in carrying a basin, a towel, and lavender bath salts. Huh? Somehow this doesn't fit the picture I have in my mind of a tea party.

Oh, but it does. In the same spirit as the Lord, who girded Himself so many years ago, this dear lady knelt before each friend and gently washed her feet with aromatic warm water and patted them dry with a soft towel all the while humming a favorite song of personal worship, giving glory to God. How humbling. How tender. How *so* like Jesus!

From a Bible commentary, I gleaned these insights as to what likely happened on Passover night in Jesus' day. According to Jewish custom, washing the feet of the head of the household was one of the duties of a foreign slave. It was never expected of a Jewish slave. However, it was a service a wife owed her husband and children their father. Since there was no servant present on the night of the Last Supper, one of the disciples should have undertaken the menial task, but none volunteered. Jesus hoped His practical demonstration would give the disciples a visual lesson that would remain with them longer than words alone.

In the symbolic act Jesus performed, only in submission could Peter have a part with Christ. "Furthermore, Peter's independent spirit and haughty attitude were inconsistent with the character of those who enjoyed sweet spiritual fellowship with their Lord in this life and who entertained the hope of enjoying eternal fellowship with Him in the world to come" (*Seventh-day Adventist Bible Commentary*, vol. 5 [Hagerstown, MD: Review and Herald Publishing Association, 2011], p. 1028). Therefore, in the act of washing someone's feet, both parties are in the perfect position to receive a blessing.

"'Then, Lord,' Simon Peter replied, 'not just my feet but my hands and my head as well!'" (John 13:9).

Let's not glance over these words too lightly and thus miss the spiritual significance. There is something special about the experience of having someone kneel before you to wash your feet, and further, if the washing is symbolically allowed to reach your heart, it gets bathed too and thus you have been renewed by the Holy Spirit and a little bit of heaven lingers on earth just for you.

I would love to have joined these ladies in their sweet fellowship. No doubt they had an unseen Guest present. No doubt

His sweet Spirit permeated the hearts of all who gathered and remained with them long after the last sip of tea.

Crowning Glory

But a woman can be proud to have long hair. Her hair is given to her for a covering. 1 Corinthians 11:15, NLV.

This piece is about hair, something "hair" today and gone tomorrow. Even though the text refers to the female gender, hopefully there is something here for every reader. Hair is something we often take for granted. We are born with some, and we'd like to keep our collection of strands all of our days. It grows rather painlessly, but it silently reminds most of us every few weeks that we need to get a trim. (I don't know how your hair lets you know, but mine does so by refusing to cooperate and becoming very unruly.) It grows and goes without our input. Most of the time, it's our decision what we choose to do with it. We shampoo it. We cut it. We curl it. We straighten it. We perm it. We shave it. Fashion, seasons, and boredom inspire us to make changes.

It so happened that today was my regular appointment to get my hair trimmed and tinted in my losing battle to turn back the waving hands of time. I opened the door to the beauty shop, intending to take a seat and relax while thumbing through mindless magazines until it was my turn, but I stopped in my tracks just inside the door. Yes, I was in the right shop, but who was doing a customer's crowning glory in place of my hairdresser? I approached slowly ... glasses would have helped clarify more quickly, but why bother? I stepped closer still. The words were organizing themselves while working their way from the back of my brain forward to my lips. *Did I have the wrong day or had my hairdresser been replaced?* And then it became clear. I was looking into the face of *my* hairdresser of twenty-something years, but she had no hair! Her thick bob had been shaved off, revealing a dark brown shadow where had once been beautiful auburn hair.

My befuddlement was not lost on either woman, and they both smiled. Over the next few minutes as my hairdresser finished foiling her customer's hair, she shared the story, which no doubt had been repeated over and over with other customers as surprised and curious as I.

You see, the hairdresser who works behind the first chair at the front of the salon is battling cancer. She continues to work when not receiving treatments, but the effect of the treatments led to the loss of her crowning glory, lock by lock. She revealed little to her coworkers in the beginning, but it was obvious to everyone what had happened the day she wore a wig to work for the first time. The presence of the wig seemed to stimulate dialogue, breaking down barriers and increasing understanding and deepening trust. They got it. They understood. She no longer felt isolated and alone among her coworkers.

What came next might have surprised her. All the ladies in the shop decided to forge their bond of solidarity in the fight against the cancer monster by shaving their hair off and embracing baldness together. They'd stand openly side by side as they worked— no wigs allowed—and Locks of Love, a nonprofit charity that makes wigs for needy Canadian and American children who have lost their hair, would benefit from their generosity. The cancer fight goes on. Hair will grow back. She and her comrades can resume choices for length, tint, and shape when the battle finishes. And may she live her life to the fullest all of her days.

Thinking about this story, I was struck by my ignorance at how hair has defined my recognition of a person. Yes, changing styles may bring on a double take, but total absence of hair created a new awareness. Hair, glasses, make-up, etc., may change our exterior, but when I came face to face with my hairdresser without hair, I was forced to look beyond the exterior for recognition. I was forced to look deeper into the face of my hairdresser, to look deeply into her eyes for recognition, for eyes will always be an open window into the hearts of those we know.

Your eyes are windows into your body. If you open your eyes wide in wonder and belief, your body fills up with light.
Matthew 6:22, MSG.

Twice Mine

As the story goes, there was a little boy who worked tirelessly to build a sailboat. At last came the day when he was ready to put her to the test. Would she float? He set her gently in the stream, stood up, and prepared to enjoy her maiden voyage, but to his dismay the wind caught her sail, tipped her over, and she was quickly sucked downstream. The little boy hurried to follow, but could not see her. She had disappeared from sight. He searched and searched, but he could not find his beloved boat. After all that loving effort, his sailboat was gone.

Some days later the boy and his mother were walking past a pawn shop in town when he glanced in the window and was shocked to see his little sailboat on display! He knew she was his, for he was familiar with her design. After all, hadn't he poured hours of love into her creation? Getting his mother's permission, he pushed open the door and approached the proprietor who stood behind the counter. "Mister" he stated, pointing to the window, "that's my sailboat."

"No it ain't," the man retorted gruffly. "It belongs to me, but if you wanna buy it I'll sell it to you for $5.00."

Five dollars! The man might as well have asked for $50.00! The little tyke didn't have two nickels to rub together. That evening the little boy approached his dad. "Daddy," he asked, "may I please have $5.00 so I can buy back my sailboat?"

Daddy was sorry his son had worked so hard on his little sailboat only to lose it, but money did not come easily, so he gave him a suggestion instead. "Son," he said, "why don't you do some chores around here, and before long you will have earned enough money to buy back your sailboat."

The little boy's eyes lit up at the idea. He'd gladly do some chores so he could buy back his sailboat. She was worth it. Before long he had earned the money he needed. Carefully he counted each coin. Yes, he had enough. Now to get back to the pawn shop and hope that his sailboat was still there! Yep. There she was in the window as if waiting for him. Pushing open the door he hastened to the counter, "Here mister," he blurted excitedly. "I have the money for the sailboat. Can I buy her?"

As he headed out the door, the owner heard him exclaim triumphantly, "I made you and I bought you. You are *twice* mine!"

This little story or parable, if you like, reminds me of the plan of salvation. In a nutshell, we were intrinsically designed by our Creator, and when our first parents chose to follow Satan over God, He could have thrown in the towel, zapped earth from existence, and started all over again. But He didn't! He loved us too much. Instead, Jesus came to pay the price for our sins, taking them upon Himself—He who had never sinned—and bore them to the cross. Three days later He arose victorious over death and sin! He paid the ultimate price to set us free!

Jesus both made us and redeemed us. We are twice His! How does it feel to be twice loved?

And from Jesus Christ, the witness, the trustworthy one, the first to come back to life, and the ruler over the kings of the earth. Glory and power forever and ever belong to the one who loves us and has freed us from our sins by his blood.
Revelation 1:5, GW.

If It Hisses …

I have never had a frightening encounter with a deadly snake before. Have you? I would imagine that if I did encounter a deadly snake in the wilderness I would instantly be filled with adrenalin and these arthritic limbs would suddenly be able to leap short buildings in a single bound! There is nothing like fear to get one moving. So what happened to Eve??

> Now the snake was the most clever of all the wild animals the Lord God had made. One day the snake said to the woman, "Did God really say that you must not eat fruit from any tree in the garden?"
>
> The woman answered the snake, "We may eat fruit from the trees in the garden. But God told us, 'You must not eat fruit from the tree that is in the middle of the garden. You must not even touch it, or you will die.'"
>
> But the snake said to the woman, "You will not die. God knows that if you eat the fruit from that tree, you will learn about good and evil and you will be like God! (Genesis 3:1–5, NCV).

The Garden of Eden must have been gorgeous, unlike anything our eyes have ever seen. It was the place where God formed Adam out of the dust of the earth and blew His breath into his nostrils and gave him life. Sadly, it was also the setting for the very first lie on earth hissed by a beautiful snake, Satan in disguise, which changed God's plan for His children.

The first lie in history is thousands of years old, and yet what is astounding is that it is still as effective today as when told to Eve. Satan is still telling the same lie today—"you won't die." You just pass from one life to the next. But what is the next life? Does anyone know exactly what it is? Is there Scripture to define it? I am a person who needs proof.

It's easy to blame the problems of the world on men, but it was the first woman who sinned. If I could have a chat with Eve, maybe it would go something like this: "Eve, you had it all. You had perfection all around you, including a drop-dead, gorgeous, hunky husband, and you walked and talked with God face to face! What could possibly make you think you could improve on that? Why listen to a *talking* snake when you had God? What on earth were you thinking?"

That snake turned out to be an impostor. We need to wake up. Be vigilant. If it hisses … back away, and fast!

Thus says the Lord of hosts: Behold, evil will go forth from nation to nation, and a great whirling tempest will rise from the uttermost parts of the earth. Jeremiah 25:32, AMP.

Transplants

This is what the Sovereign Lord says: "Will it thrive? Will it not be uprooted and stripped of its fruit so that it withers? All its new growth will wither. It will not take a strong arm or many people to pull it up by the roots. It has been planted, but will it thrive? Will it not wither completely when the east wind strikes it— wither away in the plot where it grew?" Ezekiel 17:9, 10.

I am creating new "trim" around the edge of the house by splitting up old friends; digging them up by their roots and forcing them into a new neighborhood. Plenty of water and sunshine, and hopefully they will settle in, grow, and make new friends.

I don't like to be uprooted. I don't like moving. I don't like being forced into a new community of unknowns. I am very shy, and I don't make new friends easily. My firstborn was shy too. He liked his Sabbath School class as long as we were with him. When he got a little older, it was expected that we would leave him in the careful hands of teachers to enjoy the program with other little ones. It's not easy to leave your first child in the hands of others, no matter how capable they are. We parents can be rather clingy like vines. There were tears and adjustments on my part and his, but once he settled in ... and I could let go ... he was good ... until he outgrew that Sabbath School class and needed to move on to the next.

We eventually managed to adjust back to an adult class, and we grew to enjoy the lesson study, but one day we got the announcement that the following Sabbath was going to be promotion Sabbath. Our little boy was ready to be promoted with the other children to the next class, making room for new little ones. Oh dear. We knew his pattern, and so we sat in the back row where we could keep an eye on the lobby, anticipating we would see our little tyke make his move. We didn't have long to wait. Here he came, those short legs taking long, determined strides across the lobby. He knew where to go, and he was heading back to familiar territory. Bless his sweet, little heart. Daddy scooped him up, and we loved on him and outdid ourselves in over-the-top excitement about him being big enough to go to a new class. We could have tried out for Broadway.

When I recall stories like this one, it is a bit amusing, and I can smile ... before I choke on the memory. We had no idea that our son would grow up to be so sad, that he'd make a decision to end his life—almost ending ours. We dangled by a thread for a long time. Gradually God has grown new roots for us, and we have been transplanted into a church family where we can continue to grow and even flourish a little. One can't rush growth. I think settling in to a new phase in life takes time, faith, and much patience.

See, we all have been transplanted in one way or another, whether we change jobs, move to a new location, become new parents, or lose someone dear. Some transplant decisions are not chosen; they are forced on us like I forced the change in my garden. The plants will either survive and thrive or die. Unlike them, we have hearts. We are like our Creator who made us in His image. He helps us along our journey, knowing we will experience many changes along the way. But when He returns and we at last arrive at our heavenly home, surrounded by those we love, perhaps the time we spent here on earth will soon fade into a distant memory, overshadowed by eternal bliss. This is worth longing for.

I am reminded of a sweet, old hymn "I'm Homesick for Heaven" by Henry de Fluiter. The chorus comes to mind as I prepared this piece. If you remember the tune, you are welcome to hum or sing along. Here's the chorus:

I'm homesick for heaven, seems I cannot wait,
Yearning to enter Zion's pearly gate;
There never a heartache, never a care,
I long for my home over there.

Sifting Around for Hope

We also have joy with our troubles, because we know that these troubles produce patience. And patience produces character, and character produces hope. And this hope will never disappoint us, because God has poured out his love to fill our hearts. He gave us his love through the Holy Spirit, whom God has given to us. Romans 3:3–5, NCV.

There is a world-famous daily facial moisturizer cream called "Hope in a Jar" by Philosophy. It's too pricey for my pocketbook, but I am curious about a product that claims, "Where there is hope there can be faith, where there is faith miracles can occur." It sounds nice. I wonder what it smells like? I wonder what it would feel like on my skin? Don't worry. I'm curious, but not *that* curious. Maybe it would be a total disappointment and a waste of money.

Hope cream is vastly, unspeakably different from sifting around in layers of debris searching for signs of life, signs of hope, and tragically coming up with a child, your child who has no sign of life. Just that morning he gulped down his breakfast, grabbed his book bag, and headed out the door as you blew him a kiss and told him to have a great day at school. He skipped down the sidewalk as his school bus braked to a stop. The day was off and running on normal cycle. Why would you expect this day to be any different? But sometimes a normal day turns deadly.

Today there are no street signs, no homes, no school. The land has been both swept and convulsed by a giant, writhing monster that roared through town, trashing everything in its wake and leaving unimaginable pain behind. Today is a new normal, an ugly, horrific new normal. The town claims it will rebuild into a new town. Street signs will return. Homes and schools and other buildings will take shape, but mourning will not soon end.

How do these people survive? I've heard them talk of their personal faith and looking ahead to rebuild their lives brick by brick, mortared together with hope. Real hope can't be purchased. It is something that sprouts in the heart, a solid-like faith, believing that God will supply every need. And God has been sending volunteers working around the clock to help their brothers and sisters do what they cannot do for themselves. Bless them.

Devastation is cruel. Of that, we have no doubt. We call it "mother nature," but it's more like nature turned in on itself in a fury. It's the elements God has created as the firmament (Genesis 1:8) that are disgraced by the enemy for his own cruel, heartless purpose. But we will continue to hope through our trials, growing in strength toward salvation. We will not be disappointed. Hope will hold us until we meet the God of love one day soon.

I could think of no better way to end this piece than to share two verses from John Newton's "Amazing Grace." Hum along as you read.

T'was grace that taught my heart to fear.
And grace, my fears relieved.
How precious did that grace appear
The hour I first believed.

The Lord has promised good to me.
His word my hope secures.
He will my shield and portion be,
As long as life endures.

Wake Up, Sleepyhead

Wake up, you who are sleeping. Rise from the dead and Christ will give you light. Ephesians 5:14, NLV.

My brain has been nudging me to get to the cemetery, turn the flower vase right side up, and start a season of bouquets. But what's the rush? It's not like there is a deadline. However, I guess my soul has been longing to stop by. So I hopped in the car and drove a couple miles before slowing my speed, touching the brake, and making the familiar turn into a place we have come to know. I felt that sinking feeling in my gut. Know that one? Not the choking-back-the-tears thing or the rush of nausea like I felt in the first visits, but a longing to run in and take him away with me. This longing remains.

Winter seemed extra long, and I hadn't been to the cemetery in a while. I faced the shrubbery that edges the property line, looked for the telephone pole, and then straight back. Yes, there he is. Seeing his name on bronze still chokes me. "Get up, son!" I want to shout. But I have no power. I can yell and scream and beat on the ground, but I am powerless to wake him up. He is in a deep sleep.

My mind drifts back to another time, a time when he was still with me. "Wake up, son." I nudged him gently and spoke softly close to his ear. His sleepy fragrance was sweet. He was deep in dreamland. But I couldn't let him sleep any longer. I nudged him a little harder, "Get up, son! It's your first day of school. You don't want to be late. Come on, wake up. Your breakfast is ready. Smell the toast?" His eyelids fluttered. I loved his long lashes. He grabbed the covers as he flipped over, trying to drown out his mother's pleas in favor of just a few more winks. But I was equally up to the challenge. Off with the covers. Let some cool air in. Then he stirred, blinked, rubbed his eyes and stretched with a yowling yawn. He was finally awake … barely, but enough to remember that today was the first day of school and he had to get going!

My memories replay countless events and scenarios with my children. I love letting my mind take me back to happier times. I couldn't do that for a long time. I don't remember when the first sweet memory fluttered into my awareness, when my plate had been heaped high with bitter ones for so long. But they did come … gradually. Now they sit front and center, and I enjoy their recollection. Yes, there is a bitter taste that comes after, but I *must* let the good outrun the bad.

Wrestling With God

*And He said, Your name shall be called no more Jacob [sup-
planter], but Israel [contender with God]; for you have con-
tended and have power with God and with men and have
prevailed.* Genesis 32:28, AMP.

Pain is the price we pay for admission to earth. It comes to each
of us when we least expect it. Battle weary, burdened, and in need
of rest, the trials and tragedies of life continue to overwhelm us,
draining our strength. We want to lash out. We want to blame. We
want a target for our pain. Things appear difficult, impossible in
fact, which brings a question to mind—have you ever wrestled with
God about it? Maybe your imagination can't stretch that far. But
maybe it is in prayer and conversation with Him that you wrestle
for answers and understanding. Do you think we have the right
to go to God and beat on His chest? To take Him to the spiritual
mat, as it were, and challenge Him with tough questions? I say yes
because He says yes. Sometimes God is the wrestler at Peniel.

Perhaps an explanation is in order. There is an old Bible story
about Jacob. His bio is fascinating, and you are welcome to check
it out. Meanwhile, I'd like to zero in on a portion that touches

me deeply ... in that deep soft spot where gnawing pain resides, although thankfully it is more subtle now with the passage of time. However, it is pain I must learn to live with, and I imagine you agree if you, too, have lost a beloved child.

Pain didn't start with us, however. We have to go way back to the beginning of time, and there we will find pain. Bible stories are proof enough that *to follow God is not to swagger, but to walk with a limp.* God has always used pain in the lives of those who choose to follow after Him. Pain is never our choice; it is what is chosen for us. Why? Let's see if a particular Bible story can shed some light on the topic of pain.

There are many examples to choose from, and three come readily to mind: Peter, the arrogant hot head; Saul, the violent persecutor who became Paul; and Jacob, the lying swindler who is the subject of today's story. All three men discovered firsthand that God never leaves us where we are but rather turns us into something useful for His glory. Let's pick up Jacob's story in Genesis 32. You may follow along if you like while I attempt to share a bit of his story in my own words with ideas gleaned from listening to Brian Zahnd, pastor of the Word of Life Church in Saint Joseph, Missouri, who also happens to be an excellent story teller.

Jacob was a twin. He followed his brother Esau out of the birth canal holding onto his heel, and thus, he was born a supplanter or "holder of the heel." He became a fast talker, a manipulator, a hustler. He honed his instincts to size up and use people on his way to the top. He cheated his brother out of his birthright and went on to con his uncle who conned him back. His definition of success was to swagger through life with the confidence of a con man. Life was a race, and he wanted to cross the finish line first with his backpack filled with riches.

But as it often happens, Jacob's life suddenly took a nasty turn when he got word that his twin brother was hot on his trail with murder on his mind. Jacob quickly divided his family into groups, sending them to safety, while he stayed behind to face his brother alone. He prayed that God would save him from the wrath of his brother. Alone in the darkness with the words barely out of his mouth, he was knocked to the ground by an unknown assailant. Esau? No, it couldn't be Esau. This guy was way bigger and stronger than he remembered Esau to be, but there was no time to figure out who his attacker was, for he was in for the fight of his life.

Let's "invite" Jacob to continue the story in his own words. "Down we went into the weeds and reeds, tumbling over and over in slimy mud. Who is this madman? Desperation gripped me in a cold sweat. It was hard to get a grip on this guy, but if this fight was to end in death then I was going to give it my all. My mind raced, grimly reminding me of my evil deeds, one after the other. Is this how my life will end? Will I never get to tell Esau how sorry I am for stealing his birthright?

"We fought on into the night, the silence broken only by the sounds of pounding flesh. I willed my body strength, but we were ridiculously mismatched. Clearly he could take me, so why didn't he and get it over with? *It's obvious he's playing with me*. I thought. *I'm his prey, his pawn*. Just as the foggy whisper of dawn nibbled at the edge of darkness, he made his move. It looked like a lightning bolt passed between us and zapped my hip. Searing pain like a hot knife engulfed me. I writhed in agony on the ground. Did I catch a glimpse of his face or was that pain talking? He tried to pull away now, but I clung to his neck with a grip tighter than I knew I had. I would not let go. The agony of pain was nothing compared to the agony of soul. My wretched life passed before my eyes ... it couldn't end this way. I must have a blessing. Please ... I must have his forgiveness! I was defeated, crippled for life, so would he now leave me here alone? I held on for dear life. I felt his hot breath on my neck when he finally spoke, 'Let me go, for it is daybreak.'

"I dug my nails into his skin. Through clenched teeth and with a voice strained from fatigue and pain I cried, 'I will not let you go unless you bless me.'

"Then he asked me my name. I told him. Then he said the most amazing thing, 'Your name will no longer be Jacob, but Israel, because you have struggled with God and with humans and have overcome'.

"I relaxed my grip, stunned by His words. Though in agony I could hardly wrap my mind around the blessing I had just been given. I was no longer Jacob, 'supplanter,' but Israel, meaning 'God prevails.' *How awesome.* I could scarcely take it in, but I would have plenty of time later to replay the greatest event in my life. Now I must ask Him one more question, 'Please tell me Your name?' He leaned down to my ear and softly spoke, *'Do you really need to ask?'*

"No, I didn't. My heart knew. I began to quiver with emotion from head to toe. I had wrestled with my Maker and survived to tell my story! How was that possible?"

So Jacob called the place Peniel, saying, "It is because I saw God face to face, and yet my life was spared" (Genesis 32:30). (Jacob's story was taken from verses 26--30)

Heavenly Father, as hard as it is for me to admit, and even harder to be thankful for, over time, lots of time, I have come to be thankful that You brought about pain in my life. For it was in the horrific crucible of losing my son that I truly found You. Thank You for reminding us, through Jacob's story, that it is through wrestling with You that we prevail. Amen.

Editing

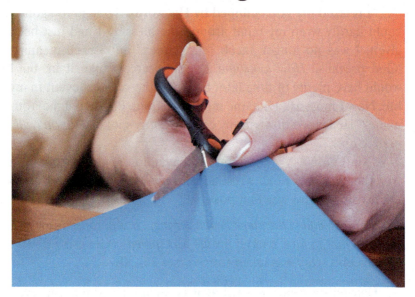

I am a fan of the long-running hit show *Everybody Loves Raymond*. I have watched the show so much that I can mute the sound and fill in the words as the pictures flicker by. If that makes me weird or ancient, so be it.

In one episode, Raymond gave the best man speech at his brother's wedding. Before that moment he was worried about what he should say, but when he stood up to speak, he said that life seems to present material. If you watched this episode, you may remember that there was drama from the usual characters, and he could have talked about all the embarrassing moments from the days leading up to the wedding, starting with his mother, but instead he talked about editing and how we can let the bad stuff fall like discarded clippings on the cutting room floor. It was a point well taken.

Have you had to edit your life story? Do you remember unnecessary drama at a wedding, even your own perhaps? How about drama at a funeral you attended? I'm familiar with that one. There was so much drama surrounding my son's death that it created bitter memories. In a previous entry I talked about "mama pain" and the need to extract the purity of our loss, separating the bad drama from our painful loss so that when we think about our loved one we do it in a way that honors them and avoids the negative thoughts that try to elbow their way into our story. We may choose to edit the dramatic moments out.

Therefore, does editing have a place in our grief journey? I say, yes, it does. May I suggest that the devil does the destroying since he is the father of lies (John 10:10)? He won't stop with just suicide if he can get others to destroy their lives too, by mixing so much family hatred in that it's hard to think of your precious child or other loved ones without additional pain.

A friend recently attended her mom's memorial service. She was naturally sad. Siblings were sad. Family members who came from near and far to attend the service were sad, too. They had lost someone they love dearly. But the time spent together was not all pleasant. There were negative family dynamics depending on whose "side" you hailed from, either the local family or the long distance family. The "sides" stayed in separate locations and did not socialize together much at all. From my standpoint as a friend and observer, I couldn't tell that there was a split in the family where each member was expected to take sides. However, my friend says that her grief triggers these painful family memories, which is probably a common occurrence in many families after loss. With editing we can choose to leave the bad stuff on the cutting room floor.

It is easy to blame others or to sabotage a gathering intended to bond us together by refusing to speak to certain family members or friends going forward. But negative thoughts or actions do us a disservice in our grief. If it serves no earthly good, then why not let it go? We deserve better.

If anyone can control his tongue, it proves that he has perfect control over himself in every other way. We can make a large horse turn around and go wherever we want by means of a small bit in his mouth. And a tiny rudder makes a huge ship turn wherever the pilot wants it to go, even though the winds are strong. So also the tongue is a small thing, but what enormous damage it can do. James 3:2–5, TLB.

Bless the Broken

They are blessed who grieve, for God will comfort them.
Matthew 5:4, NCV.

Lord, please bless the broken, the bent over, the shattered, the faint of heart. You know we are all broken from something in this life, whether from tragedy or unfortunate circumstances or disease—there are no exceptions. I long for You to visit my town and heal my brokenness. There would be standing room only in a line spanning miles and miles just to get a glimpse. You know each sorrow, each pain, each struggle, and You see each victory too. May we hope in restoration, which will come, for You have promised. Thank You for blessing those who mourn. Amen.

"There was a woman present, so twisted and bent over with arthritis that she couldn't even look up. She had been afflicted with this for eighteen years" (Luke 13:11, 12, MSG). Can you picture her? She's so bent over that her eyes face downward. All she can see are feet—hers and a few others if they happen to drift into her vision. But most likely people avoided her, assuming that she suffers from a contagious disease. Gravity and disease had twisted and pulled at her spine until she was humpbacked and living life as an outcast, if you can call that living. It had been eighteen long years! And what she wouldn't give for relief, even if only for a few minutes so she could take a deep breath, something she had not been able to do for a long time.

Suddenly she is being spoken to. Jesus did not call her name. He simply addressed her as "woman," but she knew this kind voice was speaking to her. Slowly and painfully, she walked toward the sound …

"When Jesus saw her, he called her over. 'Woman, you're free!' He laid hands on her and suddenly she was standing straight and tall, giving glory to God" (verse 13, MSG). How wonderful! How miraculous! She must have jumped for joy! The witnesses were happy for her too, but not all of them.

The self-righteous religious leaders were furious that Jesus would heal this poor woman on the Sabbath, and they shouted loud enough for everyone to hear. "'Six days have been defined as work days. Come on one of the six if you want to be healed, but not on the seventh, the Sabbath.' But Jesus shot back, 'You frauds! Each Sabbath every one of you regularly unties your cow or donkey from its stall, leads it out for water, and thinks nothing of it. So why isn't it all right for me to untie this daughter of Abraham and lead her from the stall where Satan has had her tied these eighteen years?'" (verses 14–16, MSG).

Seriously? Which one of them would have wanted to wait for healing if they were in excruciating pain? It seems like Jesus couldn't heal anyone without the Jewish leaders complaining or attempting to push Him off a cliff (Luke 4:29)! I so love Jesus' tenderness and love, but I also love His bold stance for justice, don't you? He yearned to heal people from sin and disease. But did you notice whom He blamed for this woman's affliction? He planted the blame squarely on the back of Satan.

It was the prince of darkness who bound this woman for eighteen years, and it was the Son of righteousness who set her free!

It is natural to look for a culprit when we are so broken with aching hearts. If we are looking for someone to blame for the death of a loved one, we have our answer right here. We can pin the blame squarely on Satan, for he is to blame, not God. This story was told a long time ago, but Satan hasn't changed his character. He still seeks to maim and destroy (John 10:10). And God hasn't changed His character either. He still seeks to save the lost (Luke 19:10).

There are days when I feel the enemy's boot on my back, pushing me into the dirt of life. He wants me to crack under pressure. He wants me to give up and quit. He can sneer, blow smoke from his nostrils, and push and shove, but he can't make me follow him. He knows we survivors are a force to be reckoned with when armed with the Word of God, and it makes him tremble. When we are bent over and beaten down from the cares and sorrows of life, who does not benefit from the healing touch of Jesus? All we have to do is call on His name.

He placed his hands on every one of them and healed them all.
Luke 4:40, GNT.

Where Was God?

For God so loved the world that He gave His one and only Son, that whoever believes in Him shall not perish but have eternal life. John 3:16.

I'm going to toss a direct question out there for those of you who are outliving a child. Perhaps you have asked the question either silently or openly: *Where was God when my loved one died?*

Someone whispered in my ear at the time of my son's death that God was with him when he drew his last breath. My first thought was, *Then He could have prevented it rather than allowed it.* You may have had similar thoughts. But there are always life lessons we may glean from Scripture, and perhaps we can gain understanding to apply to this very important question. The story of the crucifixion of Jesus always saddens and yet fascinates me. Where was God the Father while His Son, Jesus, was on the cross? Did He go fishing? Was He on a cosmos tour? Or was He present? Let's glean some thoughts from Scripture to capture what might have been and then see if perhaps there is a parallel application for our understanding.

Luke describes the events that transpired after Jesus died this way: "It was now about noon, and darkness came over the whole land until three in the afternoon, for the sun stopped shining. And the curtain of the temple was torn in two" (Luke 23:44, 45). Matthew adds a bit more detail: "And when Jesus had cried out again in a loud voice, he gave up his spirit. At that moment the curtain of the temple was torn in two from top to bottom. The earth shook, the rocks split" (Matthew 27:50, 51).

Around the time of Jesus' death, the veil was torn in half. To rip the veil (which was about forty-cubits or sixty-feet high) in the temple in half, someone needed to be there to tear it. And to tear it from top to bottom, someone would have to be very tall. Also, there was darkness on the earth as the sun disappeared. Looking back at the Old Testament, we discover that there was darkness when God came near to the children of Israel at Mount Sinai: "The people remained at a distance, while Moses approached the thick darkness where God was" (Exodus 20:21). So God hid Himself in darkness at Mount Sinai. Did God hide Himself in the darkness at the cross too? Did God tear the veil?

Note that there were also earthquakes in connection with God's presence: "The mountains quake before him and the hills melt away. The earth trembles at his presence, the world and all who live in it" (Nahum 1:5).

But this still does not tell us for sure where God was when His Son died, or does it? What about the story in the Old Testament when Abraham was instructed to sacrifice his son? Where was God then? Could it be a parallel to the crucifixion? Let's review the high points of this story.

It had been a long day, and Abraham was bone tired and sound asleep when his head touched the pillow, but suddenly he was wide awake. *Was that God? Did I hear a command or was I dreaming? Oh, please, may I be dreaming!* Abraham pinched himself. Ouch! That hurt! No, he was not asleep, and that was a directive from a voice he had grown to know:

"Then God said, 'Take your son, your only son, whom you love—Isaac—and go to the region of Moriah. Sacrifice him there as a burnt offering on a mountain I will show you'" (Genesis 22:2).

Not my boy, God, not my boy! I am sure Abraham pleaded

and argued in a one-sided conversation, but God spoke no more on the subject. Abraham had always obeyed God even when the request made no sense, but nothing compared to what God was telling him to do now. This was the ultimate test. Could he obey?

It must have been the longest three days in history as father and son made their way to the place where God had instructed. I am sure there was conversation, perhaps even lighthearted talk on the part of Isaac. He had often taken part in sacrifices with his dad. It was a huge part of their way of life, so this trip was not unusual ... yet.

Finally Isaac asked the hard question that Abraham knew was coming: "'Father?' 'Yes, my son?' Abraham replied. 'The fire and wood are here,' Isaac said, 'but where is the lamb for the burnt offering?'" (Genesis 22:7).

Scripture simply says that Abraham bound his son and laid him on the altar, but what a loaded sentence! Can you picture the scene? I've never been asked to point a loaded gun at my child and pull the trigger, but essentially this is what God asked Abraham to do. There would be fire and there would be death.

God was watching, no doubt about that. This was the severest test of Abraham's life, the only one of its kind in Scripture, and the relationship between God and Abraham hung in the balance— pass or fail. *Give up your only son that you love and prayed for and thought he would never be born. You must kill him to serve Me.*

The Bible says that Abraham raised the knife high in the air with Isaac watching his father's face in horror or did he have his eyes squeezed tightly shut anticipating the pain? I can't imagine more ... perhaps you can, but the picture in my mind is clear. The scene was horrific to be sure.

"But the angel of the Lord called out to him from heaven, 'Abraham! Abraham!' 'Here I am,' he replied. 'Do not lay a hand on the boy,' he said. 'Do not do anything to him. Now I know that you fear God, because you have not withheld from me your son, your only son'" (Genesis 22:11, 12).

Can we combine these two stories from both Old and New Testaments and apply them to our question for a possible view of God's relationship to His children? I think we can. A parallel story to the crucifixion is the story of Abraham and Isaac. Father Abraham was with his son the whole time, even up to the point when Isaac was about to die. Likewise, isn't it possible that God was with His Son during His agony and death? There is an obvious difference in that once Abraham passed the test, God supplied the sacrifice, but there was no substitute sacrifice at the cross. Our heavenly Father was forced to watch the agony and death of His only Son, for it took Jesus' blood to wash away our sins. What a heart-wrenching scene for God the Father to watch!

So how does this help me in my struggle? Here's a possible angle. God loves each one of His kids. He hates the sin and cruelty we endure, but He gives us total freedom to choose. The enemy pushes and prods and goads us to sin. The more kids he kills, the more he hurts God's heart. This planet is a war zone with spiritual consequences. Do you agree? There are bound to be casualties because we live with death and destruction all around us. But it is so entirely different and much worse when it happens close to home, to *our* family.

God says all things will be made plain one day. It's hard to wait, but one day we will understand in heaven. In the meantime while on this earth, we must remember that God never changes. He's always been loving and kind and good, and He always has our best interest at heart. Just as He was with Abraham through his extreme test of obedience, I have no doubt that God the Father was by His Son's side as He suffered and died. You couldn't part them, not even in the struggle to save humanity.

How priceless is your unfailing love, O God! Psalm 36:7.

IV Therapy

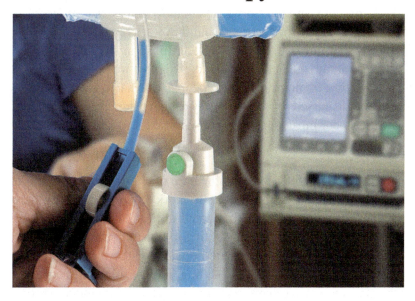

He will yet fill your mouth with laughter. Job 8:21.

Laughter may be the last thing you are interested in right now, and I understand. At least it was true for me the first months after my son passed away when grief was so raw. And the day I first laughed it shocked me. It sounded so foreign as if I had never done it before, and yet I had missed it. I don't share this to hurt myself or you but rather to embrace what is so difficult in the midst of grief. It takes a long time—no deadlines—to begin to accept that laughter is a healing balm, and it's okay to let it out. Our loved ones would want us to embrace tears of joy, even if they follow on the heels of sadness. Does that make sense?

As the years have rolled on, I have often longed to be refreshed by something funny. I have written about my cat Pipy, who always provides comic relief, and I am grateful for his antics. So this piece is intended to encourage you to enjoy a good belly laugh and not feel guilty about it. You have not "moved on" and left your loved one behind. You will always carry their memories in your heart. Trust me when I say that this doesn't happen overnight. It takes time, but when you are ready, I encourage you to embrace joy again.

In my case with the story I am about to share, I was not ready to hear it from my son's coworkers, but they were ready to share. It was unlikely that our paths would cross again, so in spite of the pain, I listened for my soul hungered for anything that would make him real at such a time of mourning. These people, who had traveled to attend the funeral, missed my son too. They couldn't stay away, and yet they felt they were intruding somehow. We tried to put them at ease by inviting them to join us for the meal after the service.

My firstborn son worked in a hospital where he repaired all kinds of equipment needed in the care of children. I was proud of his work, but I never saw him in his work environment. I had never met his coworkers until they came to the funeral to support us. They were timid at first, not wanting to intrude on our sorrow, but somehow over lunch they opened up and shared their love for my son. I was all ears. It was in this setting, sitting around the room with plates of food on our laps, that we ate and got acquainted. As they settled more easily into their chairs, they began to share stories, and I was eager to hear them. My son was quite the prankster, which I was well aware of. Of the many stories they recalled, there was one that I remember well, and I share it here in the hope that, if not today, one day you, too, will begin to remember the joyous sounds of your children loving life.

It seems there was this incident—and they all willingly put the blame squarely on my son as the culprit. The staff worked in close proximity where they charted progress notes, made phone calls, and did other office business. This particular day everyone seemed to have business to attend to elsewhere, leaving one unsuspecting teammate working at his desk all by himself. Later he said that that fact alone should have tipped him off, but he was intent on the task at hand.

And then he felt a drop on his head that made him look up at the ceiling tiles. Nothing looked amiss, so he resumed his work. Then another drop. Again he looked up at the ceiling. No cause in sight. He resumed working ... then another drop. Okay. Now he was suspicious. He was adding up the math and smelling a rat. First, his teammates were conveniently elsewhere (actually watching nearby), and second, either there was a leak right over his head or . . .

He pushed back his chair, climbed up on it where he could easily reach the ceiling tiles, and pushed one aside. Yep. Some prankster had hooked up an IV pump to drip every few seconds on his head. Brilliant.

This story made us laugh to tears ... good, refreshing tears. They laughed too, just to recall how fun our son was to work with, and were relieved that we had enjoyed the story. They would miss him. We miss him.

When we meet Jesus in the air, we will be made new, and yet we will be recognizable with the same characteristics of our original design. I am certain that my son will still have his chuckle. I am sure he and his brother will be up to their pranks again, and this time all over the cosmos. I dare to think trouble will follow these two. Good trouble, the kind that brings a smile to our faces and doubled-over laughter. I can't wait.

For what is mortal must be changed into what is immortal; what will die must be changed into what cannot die.
1 Corinthians 15:43, GNT.

Stubborn Dirt

When the dust becomes hard and the clods of earth stick together.
Job 38:38.

We have been pushed down into the dirt; we are flat on the
ground. Psalm 44:25, NCV.

You may be wondering about the title. Why write about dirt? One
could go in several directions. You pick yours, and I'll share one
from my memory bank. Many years ago I struggled to keep my two
little boys clean. It was like trying to pick up droplets of mercury.
One morning before church, after I had gotten them ready and
was putting the finishing touches on myself, I realized that it was
all too quiet. Instinct said that they were up to something. That
something turned out to be magic markers—each child had used
their sibling's face as the drawing surface. And naturally they each
had chosen dark colors to draw with. As you know there is nothing
"magic" about the color disappearing. I scrubbed and scrubbed,
stopping short of rubbing off skin, and they went to church looking
like I had beaten them. Fortunately, no one called Child Protec-
tive Services.

I have another dirty story, and this dirt was very stubborn too! After we had an old sidewalk removed and a new one put in, I set out to make our home have more curb appeal by purchasing some perennials and adding some river rock around the edges of the new flower bed. The challenge was that when I tried to dig in the dirt that had been packed under the old sidewalk in order to plant my plants, it did not want to budge an inch—no matter how hard I tried. When I banged the shovel on the surface, it sounded like rock.

I wish there weren't a spiritual application here, but sadly, we all have dirt. If not outside dirt, we have dirt inside that needs frequent cleaning. We keep dirty little secrets, and the list goes on. And if that is not bad enough, we have an enemy who loves to grind our faces in the dirt every chance he gets. When all seems dark, and my spirits are down, is when I feel my face being pressed into the dirt under his heavy boot.

We turn our thoughts toward heaven and ask, "Lord, where are You when the dirt of life is more than we can bear? Are You still fighting for us? Are You taking a mighty swing at the enemy, knocking him flat? Please kick him to the curb and surround us with Your holy warring angels, standing shoulder to shoulder so that he cannot get back in. We need protection from his boot and flying arrows." For we know that "[Satan's] arrows whiz around me" (Job 16:13, AMP).

But there is good news! Although we live in a sin-infested planet, Satan does not have the last word. He would like you and me to give him room to work in our minds and sign on the dotted line to be comrades forever, but we have a choice. Jesus also desires that we give Him permission to work in our minds and hearts by submitting to His will. He will take care of our sins one by one. And He will take care of the sin problem permanently very soon. The promise was given in the Garden of Eden after Eve and Adam sinned.

"God said, 'And I will put enmity between you and the woman, and between your offspring and hers; he will crush your head, and you will strike his heel'" (Genesis 3:15). Satan will finally get his due. At last his head will be under the heavy boot of God, and thankfully it will be an injury from which he will not recover. Praise God!

Up Close and Personal

Yep. That's Pipy. He eyes me from the floor, pausing for effect since timing is everything. *Oomph.* He jumps up on my lap, getting right in my face. First he does the head bump to my nose, sniffs to see if I've had anything interesting to eat lately, and tickles me with his whiskers as he settles down close enough to reach his paws up to knead my neck. Every ritual up to this point is tolerated because I love him, but we both know that kneading my neck is off limits, although he patiently and persistently tries.

Another anniversary looms on the horizon, and I can almost picture the "snow-capped peak" of pain rising up like the Colorado Rockies in the distance. Pipy is a reminder. He was but a pipsqueak a few years ago. Tiny, frail, and probably one or two meals shy of death when he popped out of a soybean field as we strolled by one day. He's far from skinny now and many meals could be skipped, just like his mama, but looking into his big, almond-shaped soulful eyes reminds me that I had asked my firstborn son who was visiting us one summer weekend if he'd like to take him home, but he had said, "No." Probably because of his allergies or maybe because he was already thinking … planning … and he didn't want the responsibility. Within days he died by suicide.

Flashbacks. Triggers. We all have them. Some may be mildly sensitive, but most are sharp as a tack, especially for me as the months tick off and another anniversary approaches. My heart beats faster, my palms sweat. *It's anxiety, Lord. Do You feel it too?* I am relieved when the month of memories passes, but up until then it's as if there is a distant rumble of thunder, a sense of foreboding as boiling, frothing, raging waves roll toward me, threatening to capsize me, sending me into a tailspin, as I struggle to give birth to new words in an attempt to soothe away the pain. Haven't I done that over and over already? But there is always more.

I am reminded that Someone else desires to be up close and personal. It's Jesus Christ, my Savior and Friend. I like the way He talks about the importance of friendship with His disciples in John 15.

"I have loved you the same way the Father has loved me. So live in my love. If you obey my commandments, you will live in my love. I have obeyed my Father's commandments, and in that way I live in his love. I have told you this so that you will be as joyful as I am, and your joy will be complete. Love each other as I have loved you. This is what I'm commanding you to do. The greatest love you can show is to give your life for your friends. You are my friends if you obey my commandments. I don't call you servants anymore, because a servant doesn't know what his master is doing. But I've called you friends because I've made known to you everything that I've heard from my Father" (John 15:9–15, GW).

I desire Jesus to be my best friend. I desire to love others the way He loves you and me. We humans are often a challenge to love, and I am far from His example. I have often thanked Jesus for sending Pipy at just the right time. He allows us to love him, and he loves us right back. When he wants to be right in my face, I try to understand that he is communicating with me in his language of love, often times sensing that I need extra love because I'm feeling sad.

Thank You, Jesus, for Your loving friendship. Thank You for sending Pipy to give us comic relief and love. Thank You for being both loving and persistent in wooing us into a heart-to-heart relationship with You. Amen.

Hannah's Miracle

In my distress I called to the Lord; I cried to my God for help.
From his temple he heard my voice; my cry came before him,
into his ears. Psalm 18:6.

"There was a certain man from Ramathaim, a Zuphite from the hill country of Ephraim, whose name was Elkanah" (1 Samuel 1:1). And so begins the story of Hannah, a woman whom many can relate to, who longed to have a child of her own. Elkanah had two wives, Hannah and Peninnah. You can see trouble brewing already, can't you? Apparently polygamy was ethical during this period in our world's history, and God allowed it. Of course, it was not the ideal as we shall soon see.

Peninnah had children, and Hannah could not get pregnant. Seeing Peninnah's children running around reminded her of her barrenness and caused her great pain. If that were not enough, Peninnah taunted her at every opportunity. Elkanah tried to comfort Hannah and give her extra attention, which did not go unnoticed by Peninnah, but it caused other problems, for just like Satan in heaven, "jealousy over attentions offered another, whether in the home or elsewhere, breeds a taunting, exasperating malice that finds expression in the icicle drippings of ridicule" (*Seventh-day Adventist Bible Commentary*, vol. 2 [Hagerstown, MD: Review and Herald Publishing Association, 2011], p. 455).

Hannah did not retaliate but instead gave way to quiet tears, especially at the temple. While there for worship and annual feasting, she found a quiet place and poured out her heart to God. She was sad, lonely, and desperate for a child. *Just one, God!* Then Hannah did the unthinkable to this modern mother's way of thinking anyway, she told God that if He answered her prayer and granted her a son, then she would give him back to Him as her gift for answering her prayer!

Sidebar: I can picture the scenario here. It's much more serious than my bargain prayers with God. It is embarrassing to admit that I have gone back on my promises time after time. Would I have been able to keep this promise? Would I have been able to give my son to Eli, the sanctuary guardian, and let him raise him for me? I don't know about you, but this gives me pause. And then ... NO!

God heard Hannah's prayer, and she conceived and delivered a healthy boy. They named him, Samuel, saying, "Because I asked the Lord for him" (1 Samuel 1:20). There are times when I wish Bible stories had more details and this is one of those times. I am sure there was much rejoicing in Elkanah's household except for his other wife, but the Bible does not say. It just says that Hannah told her husband of her plan. She would take Samuel to the temple after he was weaned and leave him there, forever.

Hannah did not go back on her word. She took Samuel to the temple, and he lived there with priest Eli and helped around the temple, all the while learning more about God, who was already working His plan for Samuel to one day do a great work as His prophet. There is so much to unpack in this story that you may wish to read it for yourself. Perhaps in another story we can delve into Samuel's life a bit more.

But this piece is focused on Hannah, the woman who was barren and despised by Peninnah, and yet, her story is one of faith. She put her confidence fully in God, putting her petitions before

Him and trusting in Him to answer in His perfect timing. She kept her promise to God and her husband agreed with her plan, which must have been difficult too, as the father of this little tyke.

I don't know that I could have done what Hannah did. I don't think I could take my toddler to church and leave him there for the pastor to take care of. We do things differently now, but just the sound of that is impossible to think about. But here's the clincher: Hannah totally surrendered. She held nothing back. She honored God with her promise, and it was God's privilege to grant the miracle she so desired.

Part the Water

I have no claim to fame in the swimming department. In fact, dog paddling is the only stroke I mastered … minus the stick of wood … however, a large chunk of driftwood might have kept my head above water. It is tough swimming strokes after suicide. You feel as if you have no strength. And you have no interest in life. You'd rather drown, but God then tosses you a life preserver—or driftwood—so you keep paddling, even if it is slowly.

There are many songs that come to my mind which help in the healing process—I am sure you can think of some. Their words have rich meaning, such as those that talk about God calming the storms in our lives and rescuing us from the winds and waves that threaten to engulf us.

I don't know about you, but I'm not always pleasantly floating. There are days when I am frantically paddling, kicking my feet, and taking in gulps of water. "Thanks for tossing me a piece of driftwood, Lord, but I need more," I cry. "I need Your hands under me, guiding me like a rudder to a safer depth. Maybe soon I will even touch bottom and stand upon solid ground."

"God, take my hand. Lead me to safety. I know You know everything about me and those around me. I know You know far more than I know about those I have been forced to say goodbye to. I know You know I long to understand why. I know You know I have found myself blaming You and others for his death. I know You know You can take the blame, for You took all our sins and laid them on Your one and only Son at the cross and left them there. And He arose to everlasting life, showing us the way to life eternal," I continue.

"So here is my pain, Lord. I am ready to hand it over to You, knowing You hold me up in the raging waters. Knowing You will part them and lead me safely to the shore. Knowing You are the only one who can heal me, I hand my pain to You. I choose to lean on Your everlasting arms. You love me unconditionally. I love You back. You will supply my every need, and I thank You for that. And when the storms of pain rise within me, threatening to engulf me once again, You are the Anchor for my soul. Amen."

We have this hope as an anchor for the soul, firm and secure. Hebrews 6:19.

No Claim to This Boy

Satan and his evil angels are going to burn up and be ashes under our feet. Knowing this, he is a raging lion seeking to destroy many so that he doesn't have to die alone (Revelation 20:10; Malachi 4:3; 1 Peter 5:8; John 10:10, paraphrased).

No, Satan can't claim this boy. He was prayed for all his life, he was read Bible stories as soon as he could listen, and he was educated in Christian schools. He learned that God loved him. He learned that Jesus loved him and gave up His life to pay for his sins.

In spite of every good thing we did as his loving parents, we could not keep him alive. The enemy of his soul was always trying to pull his strings. Pain—pull, pull, pull. Anger—pull, pull, pull. Poor self-image—pull, pull, pull. Depression—pull, pull, pull. He blamed God for his troubles—pull, pull, pull. He was reeled in tighter and tighter, his agony mounting. I suspect that all he could see was blackness. The string became so taut that it snapped—all he wanted was for the pain to stop—and it did.

Now he sleeps the sleep of death and is at peace (Isaiah 57:2). Satan can pull his strings no more. God is letting him rest from all his agony. He is in the sleep of death; he's taking a "dirt nap." He is resting from pain, depression, and all the disappointments he faced in his life. Some I know. Many I do not know. But God knew them all and loved him with that big heart of His as if he were the only child on earth. And it is the same for you.

No, the enemy cannot claim this boy. He was a prayed-for boy. And God hears and rewards the faith of His praying parents. I believe. I have hope. I have faith that God will do what He promises. After all, "will not the Judge of all the earth do right?" (Genesis 18:25).

Who can keep us away from the love of Christ? Can trouble or problems? Can suffering wrong from others or having no food? Can it be because of no clothes or because of danger or war? The Holy Writings say, "Because of belonging to Jesus, we are in danger of being killed all day long. We are thought of as sheep that are ready to be killed." But we have power over all these things through Jesus Who loves us so much. Romans 8:35–37, NLV.

You will live secure and full of hope; God will protect you and give you rest. Job 11:18, GNT.

Who Knows Best?

One of my boys had a general dislike for anything he hadn't yet tried in his young life—which was a laundry list. He was not easily convinced either. There was the usual bartering at the table. You know the drill, "finish your peas before you can play." I never tried the one "you will finish your oatmeal even if it takes all day." Even if I had tried it, he was born a politician so he probably would have had a comeback line. Cherub politicians with cute dimples are hard to resist.

He was just a little tyke when I thought for sure he would need no persuasion to try a piece of fresh, fragrant, mouth-watering (to his parents, that is) apple pie. Nope. "What's in it?" was always his question. Here we go again. He asked the same question about chili, which he happened to like, but he disliked beans and what's the main ingredient in most chili recipes? I had to get creative in my answers to keep him eating the stuff. But I was not prepared to be grilled over something as nice as pie.

He persisted in his resistance, convinced he wouldn't like it. No matter how many spoonfuls I brought to his lips, he clamped his teeth together. Well, it wasn't good-for-you green vegetables so why create anxiety in the poor little chap? Dessert is optional, right? I should've been pleased. Besides, every bite he refused became mine to enjoy. Until he weakened a little ... Perhaps his curiosity got the best of him, and with the very last bite, he opened his mouth and I spooned it in. I wish I had a picture of his face. He lit up like a Christmas tree. It was an instant hit, and he clamored for more. Sorry, buster, pie's all gone.

All the next week he badgered me. "When are you going to make more apple pie, Mommy?" he fired at me about every hour. He counted down the days until the weekend. The questions continued even through church. "Shhh, son, no pie until we get home," I whispered. It was too much for a wiggly little boy to take. No sooner had the preacher said "Amen" when out of the mouth of this babe, and loud enough to echo across the aisle, came, "Now I can have some apple pie!" Yes, you can little one. Yes, you can.

That story will forever bring a smile to my face and probably color to his cheeks if he knew I shared it. But his selective nature, or better yet, his stubborn nature, reminds me of, ahhhhhh, me. Sometimes I think I know best. Ever found yourself in that spot, spiritually speaking? Never? Ah, come on, mate. Humility is a sign of progress.

To make a spiritual point, our first mom, Eve, thought she knew better, but she was foiled by the master of evil himself. This was not a job for one of his demon angels. Oh, no. This gig could not risk mismanagement. All the other worlds had sent them packing, and they weren't ready to retire. They needed work to do and people to do it with, so earth had to be a success.

The plan was simple and yet complex. First, the enemy hoped to lure Eve away from her husband and toward the part of the garden God had cautioned them to stay far away from to avoid temptation. So that is where Satan, disguised as a dazzling serpent, had coiled himself around a tree limb and peeked through the branches in a stakeout set for Eve.

If you take away nothing else, remember this: never argue with the devil. Let God do battle with him. Instead of engaging in conversation as Eve did, tell him to "get behind me" just as Jesus did when He was tested in the wilderness (Matthew 16:23). Eve found herself alone at the tree. She was curious about a talking snake, so she paused to listen and was drawn in by his charm. Then he engaged her in conversation by asking a question about God's fairness. This portion of Genesis is so complex that we each should take it line by line in study because history does repeat itself. May we learn lessons from those who have gone before us, note the mistakes that caused them to fall, and avoid the pain and agony they suffered.

Now the serpent was more crafty than any of the wild animals the LORD God had made. He said to the woman, "Did God really say, 'You must not eat from any tree in the garden'?" Genesis 3:1.

Sunday Is Coming!

It's time for a wardrobe change. At last the earth sheds her thick white blanket and sends up tiny green shoots to stitch together a fresh new frock for Spring. Birds chatter the news of the day while they busy themselves with nest details. Trees and flowers already show signs of promise with their loaded brushes poised to paint the landscape in fresh pastels. I look down at the mat under my feet. It, too, has shed its drab brown. This is our land, of sorts. We bought a piece of it—albeit kicking and flailing in protest. It seems we had no choice. Someone we loved dearly ended his short life and needed a place to rest under a blanket of green.

As I stand here surveying the signs of spring, my mind wanders to a quiet Saturday outside Jerusalem. The horrendous beatings, fake trials, shouting and sobbing at the foot of the cross had all passed. Friends and family had quietly laid Jesus to rest in a borrowed tomb. They would return after the Sabbath hours to embalm Him, as was their custom, but now was the time to mourn their loss. He had done what He came to do. Jesus had predicted that He would rise in three days, but those words had slipped from memory (John 2:19). He was her Son, their Master, and their Lord, and now He was dead. Sunday was on its way. It would come right on time, just as Jesus had promised. Now it was Saturday, and it appeared to be never-ending, stretching to eternity as far as they knew. How would they go on without Him?

Heaven had a different point of view. As horrible as it must have been to watch "the plan" stretch out before them, the excitement was building. The Father's heart beat faster. The angels milled around the throne obviously waiting for the moment to come. Gabriel was at his post, keeping his eyes on the Father. It would be his most important assignment ever, and he was ready. Eternity's clock ticked toward the appointed hour. Inside the tomb all was quiet. The Savior had completed His work of saving mankind. His trust had always been in His Dad. He was not ticking down time. His job was over. He was sleeping the dreamless sleep of death.

Gabriel tried not to "bug" his Maker with intent staring, but he was eager to get going. However, God would give the signal right on time, and when He did, Gabriel would move faster than the speed of light. As the black of night gave way to the first hint of red, Gabriel flexed his rippling muscles. He got the signal! Now! He bolted through the cosmos encased in the bright beams from his Father's face. Heaven hushed. No one dared breathe. God leaned forward in eager anticipation. The angels leaned forward, too.

Gabriel ripped through space trailed by lightening, breaking the sound barrier as he went. As his feet touched down in front of Jesus' tomb, the light from heaven temporarily blinded the Roman guards who fell down like dead men. The earth trembled and rocked on its axis as an earthquake shook awake sleeping saints.

Gabriel rolled back the stone as if it were a pebble. In a voice that rumbled on earth, but was heard as the sweetest music in the throne room of heaven, Gabriel cried, "Jesus! Son of God, wake up! Your Father calls You!"

Sunday had come! The bleak darkness of Saturday had passed forever from view for Jesus was alive!

For those of us on earth who have lost a loved one, it seems as if "Sunday" will never come. Death follows life as it always has. Will it ever end? Will we ever stop putting new bouquets of flowers on our son's spot, like other families? Will Saturday's gloomy grip ever be broken? Yes! Sunday is coming!

And Sunday—whether it be Monday, Tuesday, or any other day of the week as we know it—will come. Relief is speeding toward us with the Deliverer slated to be right on time. Jesus will return! He will wake up His sleeping children just as He promised! The Creator of life broke the cycle of sin on the cross and conquered death. Eternity is real! Families who have mourned many dark Saturdays will soon forget the pain of loss when Eden is restored. Loved ones will embrace and eternity will be ours forevermore.

For God so loved the world that He gave His only Son. Whoever puts his trust in God's Son will not be lost but will have life that lasts forever. For God did not send His Son into the world to say it is guilty. He sent His Son so the world might be saved from the punishment of sin by Him. Whoever puts his trust in His Son is not guilty. Whoever does not put his trust in Him is guilty already. It is because he does not put his trust in the name of the only Son of God. John 3:16–18, NLV.

Baby Laughter

Is anything too hard for the Lord? Genesis 18:14.

Sarah shall bear you a son; and you are to name him Isaac [he laughs]. Genesis 17:19, GW.

Isaac was a darling baby boy. His name was extra special because God had chosen his name. Mom and Dad didn't care—they were still too stunned at the very prospect of having a baby of their own. He would be their only child. But let's drop back and pick up the story.

How in the world could a baby be conceived at their age? They were dumbfounded at the news even though it had been hand delivered from heaven. Sitting at the table, Sarah could hear the conversation outside around the campfire. With just animal skins separating her from the conversation, she could clearly hear what was being said. So startled by the thought, and probably in denial, she laughed at the very idea. I probably would have too, to be honest. After all, Sarah was no spring chicken.

The Bible tells us in Genesis that Sarah was ninety and her husband ninety-nine years of age when it was announced that they were finally to be parents. Long before, God had told Abraham that he would have so many descendants that they would resemble grains of sand on the seashore. At that point they were both young and full of life so the thought of being parents "soon" filled them with joy. But the joy began to evaporate as the years rolled on.

Can you picture yourself pregnant at the age of ninety? Stooped, wrinkled, and tottery, Sarah was about to trade in her walker for a stroller and deliver her child on the geriatric ward. How absurd! Paparazzi would be camped outside the hospital for days in advance, and the story would fill the tabloids with book and movie deals in the works. What a picture!

I would imagine it took these soon-to-be parents time to adjust to the news long after their visitors left. Pondering his name ... Isaac, which means laughter ... God knew their reaction and that Sarah would laugh. Perhaps there is a connection? At any rate they would never forget this day or the ones to follow—providing Alzheimer's disease did not sneak up on them.

I did not pick out baby names based on the origin, did you? But back in those days, they did. I have since looked up the meaning of the names of my children, and it is something to ponder.

This story may be humorless for you today. You may be too close to loss to be impacted by humor. I understand. I recall when I could neither listen to music nor did I have any thoughts or pictures in my mind that weren't laced with bitterness and pain. If you are there, I am so sorry for your suffering. We have a time of it, don't we? But if my journey in any way mirrors yours, I can tell you that time—lots of time—will eventually bring back some sweetness to soften the bitter edges of your life. I think tragedy is forever bittersweet; I suspect it is a given, but time helps us focus on the bigger picture. Somehow we go on. We travel with those who have similar experiences, and we lean on the Lord for strength.

Perhaps an important point of this treasured story is that Abraham and Sarah had given up. They had lost all hope of becoming parents and even decided to take matters into their own hands instead of waiting on God to deliver on His promise. You can read the interesting twists in this "soap opera" story in the book of Genesis. It's a page turner. But God never promises what He cannot deliver. When it became obvious that conception would be a miracle, God stepped in and the impossible became possible, right on time. Baby Isaac was a miracle baby. I am sure his parents often told him about his beginnings, and his story was recorded for all of us to read and be reminded that we need never give up on God—He coaxes and encourages us to cling to His promises of hope.

Be strong and let your heart take courage, all you who wait for and hope for and expect the Lord! Psalm 31:24, AMP.

Another Fish Story

My firstborn son was the angler in our family. My children were very young when introduced to the fine art of fishing for fun—catch and release. They got into it and made many canoe trips down lakes and rivers seeking the best and biggest fish for bragging rights. Maybe in heaven they will get to pick up where they left off.

When I think about my children fishing, I think about the disciples and Jesus and the many fishing stories that are told in the Gospels. For instance, read this account in John: "After this, Jesus appeared once more to his disciples at the Sea of Galilee. This is how it happened. Simon Peter said to the others, 'I am going fishing.' 'We will come with you,' they told him. So they went out in a boat, but all that night they did not catch a thing" (John 21:1–3, GNT).

Keep these few texts in mind as we slightly shift gears, and I ask you a few questions. If someone were to ask you to give a physical description of Jesus' appearance, how would you imagine Him? Would you picture Him as a baby in a manger with a sunbeam over His head? Or does the image of an emaciated Jesus suspended on a cross with blood running down His side, deathly pale and gaunt, with His eyes looking heavenward, come to mind?

I'm not condemning either picture or the artists who have portrayed Jesus in this manner, but could there be others?

According to what I read in the Gospels, Jesus had muscle. After all, didn't He flip over tables, sending coins tumbling and money changers scrambling? He showed His temper too, didn't He? Well, what about the possibility of a playful Jesus? Does that seem rather out of place? Do you think He and His disciples ever laughed during the three years they were together? Just for fun, let's explore a fish story tucked inside the book of John in the Gospels. There were several fish stories, but let's explore the one in John 21, and once again, let's add a generous helping of imagination ...

It was late. The Sea of Galilee was as smooth as silk, and it beckoned. It had been a rough few days, and the boys were exhausted. Their Master had been tortured and executed by crucifixion, and they either watched or ran. They had left their livelihood and families behind to follow when He had invited. Apparently His mission had been accomplished, and theirs would soon begin ... without Him. They needed some time to unwind. What better way than to go fishing?

"I'm going to take Dad's boat out and cast some nets. You in?" Peter tossed out the question as the guys polished off a late meal this moonlit night.

"Yeah, let's," they chorused.

There's nothing like going fishing to clear your head. But other than some good conversation with intermittent dozing throughout the night, the sea kept her secret stash. They did not catch a single fish all night long. Bummer. Now it was dawn and muscles ached from being scrunched in tight positions; their bodies clamored for a good stretch. Perhaps it was time to pack it in.

Their whereabouts was not unknown to the beachcomber on the shore. He kept an eye on His friends as He grilled breakfast. From the distance and in the foggy morning mist, the guys saw a lone figure on the beach, but that was common. They didn't suspect it was Jesus, and He didn't bother to clear their vision. He took pleasure in keeping His identity a secret for the moment.

Jesus had been turning the fish on the grill, but now He rose to

His feet and stretched. He watched His mates intently while chewing on a piece of grass. He knew they had caught nothing. Tossing the grass, He cupped His hands around His mouth and called out to the fisherman, "Catch anything?"

Peter yelled back, "Naw. Lousy night."

Jesus could have staged a show-stopping, pyrotechnic display to arrest their attention and fill the heavens with fireworks, but that was not His style, not at birth and not now. Instead, we see a side of Jesus probably only known to the disciples who were with Him day and night for three years—a playful side that loved to do the unexpected, bringing happiness to those around Him. Here was one of those moments where Jesus let the drama play out, no doubt savoring every moment.

Now the beachcomber hollered, "Why don't you cast your nets on the right side?"

What? Who had said that to them before? Who else could it be but their Lord! Smiles broke across their faces like the dawn. It's Jesus! They hustled to cast the nets, anticipating what would happen—just like old times. In seconds the nets were bursting with a writhing catch. With biceps bulging and backs straining, they hauled the catch into the boat, and before it could sink and they lost it all, they headed for shore. Of course, impatient Peter couldn't wait that long, so he dove in and swam to shore. Dragging his soggy body unto the beach, he grabbed Jesus in a wet bear hug. Can you picture it?

The rest of the disciples pulled the boat up on shore. They'd count the fish later. Their bellies were empty and the smell of grilling fish hit their noses. Yum. Breakfast fit for a king and cooked to perfection by the King! How wonderful to see their Master again. They took turns grabbing Him in bear hugs. This was the third surprise visit since His resurrection, and they loved it. Although still not fully comprehending all that had taken place, it was slowly sinking in. They were learning they could put their full trust in Jesus.

With bellies full, they relaxed around the fire—sometimes chattering, sometimes silently lost in their private thoughts. The boys knew Jesus would soon return to heaven to carry out His work from there while they took up the mantle and carried the Good News far and wide. They had gotten to know Jesus, and by getting to know Him, they had met His Dad, for Jesus had said, "If you have known me, you will also know my Father. From now on you know him through me and have seen him in me" (John 14:7, GW).

Ideas for this story came from *Beautiful Outlaw* by John Eldredge. It is a wonderful book about the unexpected, playful, light-hearted side of Jesus' personality. It's so human, so real, so not religious; a far cry from the serious, stoic Jesus we usually read about. I can't do this story justice, but if it creates a thirst in you for more and you choose to read the book for yourself, you won't be disappointed.

We can add one more tidbit to this playful side of Jesus. Fishermen do not dally when hauling their catch to shore. You can't sell stinky fish, so the boys knew they had delayed this chore long enough. "We'd better get the catch counted, boys," one of them stated.

"Yeah," called another, "we'd better," as they unwound their bodies and got to their feet.

Jesus, squinting into the sunshine, spoke up softly, "There are one hundred and fifty-three."

Oh, yeah, right. We have Jesus with us. No need to count this catch.

There had to be high fives, back slaps and grins all around. They were a band of brothers who personally knew the King.

I have a picture of a fishing boat hanging on my wall that reads: "Cast your net with all the might of your faith into the waters of His will. Send it deep into the sea of His promises, into the waters of His abundance, into the depths of His supply. As you do, you will gather—more wonders than you have ever seen, more surprises than you can ever imagine, more blessings than you can ever hold." ~Roy Lessin

Love Cups

The greatest need in the world is love. To quote author Kay Kuzma from a sermon she delivered on September 21, 1996, "Love is our basic need. We're all very much like 'love cups.' When we're full to overflowing, we have enough love to give away. But when we're empty we are miserable. We so often try to fill ourselves up. We equate love with attention. So often when we feel empty, we do crazy things like show off, or gossip, or put other people down so we look better. We have a way of trying to get some kind of attention. And yet what often happens is instead of getting filled up, we get emptied."

Bailey is our love-cup cat. He doesn't like to be held. He wants his feet on terra firma. Be warned. If you pick him up, he'll squeal like a pig! His favorite thing is to be petted while lying on the carpet. We have wood floors with accent rugs. I know when he has an "itch needing scratching" because he will make a little sound (sorry, can't put into words) and make a beeline for a piece of carpet. You can hear when he plops on his side because he sounds like he has just knocked the wind out of himself. Now it's time to paint a picture—you know—the thousand-word kind?

Bailey rolls around on his back, occasionally looking up to see if I have gotten the message yet. If he sees me coming, he puts his head back down and waits for me to stroke his belly, scratch his ears, and rub his head. He gets his diesel motor going, which sounds like it's way overdue for a tune up. He's just getting his love cup filled to overflowing. But he must leak a little, because throughout the day this scene is repeated over and over. Gotta love the little guy. Bending over is good exercise for me too. So it's a win/win.

The following scriptures are two of my favorites. If you put them together, they say something like this to me: I made you with an eternity-sized hole in your heart that nothing can fill but Me. I want you to crave Me like I crave you. Let's spend time together like best friends do. As we love each other, you will see that I am the only One you need. Yes, My child, you are complete in Me.

It is beautiful how God has done everything at the right time.
He has put a sense of eternity in people's minds.
Ecclesiastes 3:11, GW.

And God has made you complete in Christ.
Colossians 2:10, GW.

Everything of God gets expressed in Him, so you can see and
hear Him clearly. You don't need a telescope, a microscope, or a
horoscope to realize the fullness of Christ, and the emptiness of
the universe without Him. When you come to Him, that fullness
comes together for you, too. His power extends over everything.
Colossians 2:10, *MSG*

Quiet ... For Now

It was a beautiful fall day to take a walk, so I decided to go change the flowers on my son's grave. I made a mental note that I would pull out the bright sunflowers, dump out the rainwater that has collected in the vase, and stick in another bouquet with bright shades of red, yellow, and a touch of blue for contrast fit for fall. One thing I can still do for my son is make bouquets from silk flowers, tape them at the bottom, and add them to my growing collection to change out every season. I paused to remember ... and turned away with a tear.

Usually when I have these moments I am alone, just me and God. But today the parking lot was full. There was a service about ready to begin in one of the mausoleums. Family and friends had gathered and were chatting in little groups in the parking lot. I moved my car to the end of the lot, hoping to get out of their way since I planned to stay longer and take a walk.

There is Apostle Street, Cross Street, and a lot of other appropriately named streets as I walked along. Our son is on Prayer Street. Again, appropriate. Cemeteries are sad places. White flags are everywhere, a reminder that there are always more fresh graves under a blanket of straw and seed—little seedlings are protected and kept warm until they poke their little heads up through the straw to make a pretty green carpet to walk on. I paused to read the names etched in granite. It's become a habit of mine. Sometimes I find one I know. There is something solemn about reading the names of the deceased and also family names of those who have planned ahead and will be buried beside their loved one when their time comes. Each has a story: a beginning full of promise and an end. That's life as we know it.

The heavy equipment used to dig the spaces is parked discreetly out of view. Soon it will be used again. Family and friends will gather to say goodbye to someone they love. It's a pattern we have come to accept as "normal" ever since our first parents, Adam and Eve, bet on the sneaky snake and lost.

But there is hope! Soon this cemetery and all the others around the globe will be very active, noisy places. Jesus will call His children awake—I don't imagine it will be quiet that day! I probably won't be doing flower changes either, and no need! But if I'm alive, I'd love to run to the cemetery to watch my beloved son come back to life! I can hardly imagine how it will be, and I can hardly wait!

"Come On, Ring Those Bells"

I blew the dust off an old Christmas CD and hit the play button. As the first few notes filled the space around me, goose bumps chased one another up and down my body, and tears threatened to spill down my cheeks. I knew I was taking a risk with my emotions since the upcoming holidays will forever be bittersweet. Perhaps you, too, will be missing precious feet under your kitchen table this Christmas. But still I couldn't resist listening once again. Maybe Evie could help put a little joy into my limp holiday mood.

I closed my eyes and was instantly transported to a scene with me behind the wheel of our old Ford station wagon with two wiggly youngsters strapped down in the back seat, their heads bobbing to the tune as they joined Evie and belted out the chorus, "Come on, ring those bells."

This was our ritual song and favorite CD whenever we headed anywhere during the days before Christmas. My boys loved this song. I did too, and I still do. But it takes me back. Takes me back to the days when I had two youngins' at the supper table yelling in chorus, "Mom, he touched me!" I'll be the first to admit it … that sentence short-circuited my buttons then, but now it brings a smile to my face. I can't go back, but if I could freeze-frame that picture, I would. If I could erase the pain of suicide death, I would. Like I said, we will be missing someone precious at our table again this year.

This song, which was written by Andrew Culverwell, is intended to remind us of the happiest event on earth, the most joyous moment in history when Jesus was born. May you enjoy listening to your timeless favorites, and may you find the reason for the season even if you, too, are missing feet under your table this year.

Remember to praise his work, about which people have sung. Job 36:24, NCV.

He Knows Everything

Children like these are part of the kingdom of God.
Mark 10:14, GW.

I recall an incident that happened when my children were "knee high to a grasshopper." The younger had been punished for obeying his older brother instead of his parents, and as a consequence for his actions, he had received some "knowledge applied to his seat of understanding." Afterwards, I cuddled him and explained why his actions were unacceptable. Between heaves and sobs, he blurted out, "But Mommy, he knows *everything* and I know nothing!"

Although this precious memory happened long ago, it remains fresh in my mind and makes me smile. They were precious words out of the mouth of my babe. As the younger child, he idolized his older brother, who from his tender viewpoint could do no wrong. He loved him, was in awe of his knowledge, and trusted him to always play fair. I quickly pointed out the problem with following someone who may be a bit older but not wiser, for his counsel was often intended to get his younger brother into trouble in the first place. And of course in this situation he had taken the bait.

This story reminds me of my relationship with God. He *does* know everything, and I know very little. He can be trusted to look out for my best interests. He loves me unconditionally. Fortunately, He is willing to teach me what He knows from His Word. No matter where I pick up and read, the Bible always has something to teach me. Even a well-worn text will often smack me between the eyes as if I am reading it for the first time. Unlike childish behavior and trickery, He always has my best interest at heart.

As humans we are all broken from sin. We all are broken from tragedy of some kind, and we desire healing. The process is slow, but thorough, if left in the hands of God. He is the healer of broken hearts. He can pick up the pieces of broken relationships, broken bodies, and broken hearts and put us back together again.

Heal me, O Lord, and I shall be healed; save me, and I shall be saved, for You are my praise. Jeremiah 17:14, AMP.

Oh, the depth of the riches of the wisdom and knowledge of God! How unsearchable his judgments, and his paths beyond tracing out! Romans 11:33.

If you would like to contact Gracie,
you can reach her by visiting her blog titled
"Hope After Suicide": hopeispossible.wordpress.com

Also by Gracie Thompson:

"Shattered by Suicide:
My Conversations with God
After the Tragic Death of My Son"

from Innovo Publishing

We invite you to view the complete
selection of titles we publish at:

www.TEACHServices.com

Scan with your mobile
device to go directly
to our website.

Please write or email us your praises, reactions, or
thoughts about this or any other book we publish at:

TEACH Services, Inc.
P U B L I S H I N G
www.TEACHServices.com ● (800) 367-1844

P.O. Box 954
Ringgold, GA 30736

info@TEACHServices.com

TEACH Services, Inc., titles may be purchased in bulk for
educational, business, fund-raising, or sales promotional use.
For information, please e-mail:

BulkSales@TEACHServices.com

Finally, if you are interested in seeing
your own book in print, please contact us at

publishing@TEACHServices.com

We would be happy to review your manuscript for free.

CPSIA information can be obtained at www.ICGtesting.com
Printed in the USA
LVOW02s0429180615

442649LV00003B/3/P